BETWEEN UMNO
AND
A HARD PLACE

Research for Social Advancement
Kuala Lumpur, Malaysia

REFSA is an institute dedicated to intellectual interaction and open discussion on social, economic and contemporary issues affecting Malaysians.

We aim to conduct independent and forward-looking policy research, with a specific focus on institution monitoring. The purpose of this research is to inform society on the issues that are relevant to them, and to communicate these ideas for policy influence through their accessibility, accuracy and relevance

Institute of Southeast Asian Studies
Singapore

The Institute of Southeast Asian Studies (ISEAS) was established as an autonomous organization in 1968. It is a regional centre dedicated to the study of socio-political, security and economic trends and developments in Southeast Asia and its wider geostrategic and economic environment. The Institute's research programmes are the Regional Economic Studies (RES, including ASEAN and APEC), Regional Strategic and Political Studies (RSPS), and Regional Social and Cultural Studies (RSCS).

ISEAS Publishing, an established academic press, has issued more than 2,000 books and journals. It is the largest scholarly publisher of research about Southeast Asia from within the region. ISEAS Publishing works with many other academic and trade publishers and distributors to disseminate important research and analyses from and about Southeast Asia to the rest of the world.

BETWEEN UMNO AND A HARD PLACE

The Najib Razak Era Begins

Ooi Kee Beng

Research for Social Advancement
Kuala Lumpur, Malaysia

Institute of Southeast Asian Studies
Singapore

First published in Singapore in 2010 by ISEAS Publishing
Institute of Southeast Asian Studies
30 Heng Mui Keng Terrace
Pasir Panjang
Singapore 119614
E-mail: publish@iseas.edu.sg
Website: http://bookshop.iseas.edu.sg
ISEAS ISBN 978-981-4311-28-1 (soft cover)
ISEAS ISBN 978-981-4311-29-8 (E-book PDF)

For distribution in all countries except Malaysia.

Co-published for distribution in Malaysia only by REFSA
4A, Jalan Sepadu, Taman United, Off Jalan Klang Lama,
58200 Kuala Lumpur, Malaysia.   Website: http://refsa.org

DS597.2 O622   2010

Perpustakaan Negara Malaysia   Cataloguing-in-Publication Data
Ooi, Kee Beng, 1955-.
   Between UMNO and a hard place: the Najib Razak era begins / Ooi Kee Beng
      Includes index
      1. Political parties--Malaysia.   2. Malaysia--Politics and government.
      I. Title.
      320.9595   .

REFSA ISBN: 978-967-5942-00-6

Cover Design, Content Format and Typeset by REFSA
Printed by Vinlin Press Sdn Bhd (25680-X)
No.2, Jalan Meranti Permai 1, Meranti Permai Industrial Park, Batu 15,
Jalan Puchong,47100 Puchong, Selangor Darul Ehsan.

CONTENTS

ACKNOWLEDGEMENT

The thing about political analysis, especially of an excessively politicised country like Malaysia, is that one has to depend on the insights of others, on the bravery of staff working for print and web newspapers, on the openness of certain institutions and on the willingness of political insiders to share their thoughts.

It is to all these courageous people I acknowledge my debt. Much of what is included in this volume would not have been possible without the cyber-world synergy that the dedication of a host of people generated. I am honoured to be a part of this brew of ideas that searches persistently for new ways of solving and dissolving the many problems that Malaysia faces today.

This is dedicated to all those who write on the politics of Malaysia because they have to, and because they believe the country deserves a better future than the one now looming.

OOI KEE BENG

ABBREVIATIONS

Bersih	— *Bersih (Coalition for Free and Clean Elections)*
BN	— *Barisan Nasional (National Front)*
DAP	— *Democratic Action Party*
Gerakan	— *Parti Gerakan Rakyat*
Hindraf	— *Hindu Rights Action Force*
IMP	— *Independence of Malaya Party*
ISA	— *Internal Security Act*
MACC	— *Malaysian Anti-Corruption Commission*
MCP	— *Malay(si)an Communist Party*
MIC	— *Malaysian Indian Congress*
MCA	— *Malaysian Chinese Association*
NEP	— *New Economic Policy*
PAS	— *Parti Islam SeMalaysia (Pan-Malaysian Islamic Party)*
Petronas	— *Petroliam Nasional Berhad (National Petroleum Limited)*
PKR	— *Parti KeAdilan Rakyat (People's Justice Party)*
PPP	— *People's Progressive Party*
PR	— *Pakatan Rakyat (People's Pact/People's Alliance)*
SIS	— *Sisters in Islam*
TI-CPI	— *Corruption Perception Index by Transparency International*
UMNO	— *United Malays National Organisation*

Public Space is a Good in Itself

By Tengku Razaleigh Hamzah,

Former Finance Minister and

MP for Gua Musang, Kelantan

Anyone watching Malaysia over the last few years would have realised that its nation building is in a cul-de-sac. The legacy of mismanagement has become undeniable.

Luckily for us, this is also a time when the Internet is providing concerned Malaysians with avenues for airing their views on political, economic and social matters. More than that, it has made it possible for information and opinions published outside the country to become easily available to the common Malaysian, be he living in a kampong or next door to the Petronas Twin Towers.

This spontaneous free flow of information is the biggest challenge faced by governments that have things to hide, and who fear open discussion. These may be individual and institutional incompetence, misuse of power, corruption, vested interests, you name it.

As we very well know, things kept in the dark tend to fester, and too long now, that is how politics is done in Malaysia. Information is not considered the property of the common man; his right to have.

This is changing fast, and it is good that so many of us are now participating in this new culture of openness. What belongs to us, we have to claim and not wait for it to be given us.

Now, information is not only about facts and details. That is only part of it. Equally important is the analysis of these facts and details. In all issues, facts and details are never complete, and their significance and relevance are never obvious at first sight.

That is why we have public intellectuals; that is why we now have citizen journalists and freelancers; that is why we have bloggers; that is why we have newspapers; that is why we have non-governmental organisations, that is why we have the opposition.

Openness is good in itself.

Bits of truth manifest themselves in the public sphere when people are able to voice their ideas, their feelings and their hopes. And as we like to say, grains of sand will make a mountain.

This building of a mountain through little grains of sand is accelerated in our time by the amazing information technology now let loose upon the world. More and more of our young and not-so-young, whether they live in Malaysia or outside its borders, are now able to participate in the public space that now extends uncontrollably beyond our geographical confines.

This is all for the better.

I have known Dr Ooi Kee Beng for over five years now. He came to my office to interview me about my views on the late Tun Dr Ismail Abdul Rahman in 2005, and I remember hoping that his book would do justice to the great man's legacy. I need not have worried. *The Reluctant Politician* captured Tun Dr Ismail's ideas most professionally for a new generation of Malaysians to ponder over.

But of equal interest to me have been Kee Beng's many piercing comments on Malaysian politics made over those five years. These were printed on websites, in regional newspapers and in three collections published during Abdullah Badawi's period (*Era of Transition; Lost in Transition;* and *Arrested Reform*).

This present collection of over 40 articles covers the end of the Abdullah period and provides us with a penetrating analysis of the first year of Najib Abdul Razak's administration. But more than that, what the reader of these articles comes away with is intimate knowledge of the many issues that the new prime minister will have to face in the near future, and the many challenges that the country can no longer ignore in the era of expanding public space.

In the end, all of us may gripe about the past, and even the present. But the future is our responsibility, and my belief is that it is best taken through open debate and fearless discussions.

A Rocky Beginning

The post-Mahathir period in Malaysia continues. The first person saddled with dismantling the Mahathir legacy – Abdullah Badawi – showed promise in the beginning but ended up a failure where the reversal of governance deterioration was concerned.

Even after voters threw out his coalition in four northern states (aside from the perpetually oppositional Kelantan), he chose to stay put. However, his lack of initiative continued to whip up support for the opposition. His appointment of Zaid Ibrahim to reform the legal system failed dismally with the latter resigning over grave differences with other members of his conservative cabinet.

Finally, in desperation, his party's supreme council moved against him. On April 3, 2009, Najib Abdul Razak took over as prime minister. He thus became the second to be saddled with cleaning up the mess left by Mahathir.

The chapters included in this book trace the issues and problems that plagued his first year in office. How he chose to act, and how his party chose to act, in each individual case, provides valuable information about this new premier.

Although Najib has been in politics since his father, Tun Abdul Razak Hussein, passed away in January 1976, how he would perform as the country's top politician in these critical times was never quite certain.

True, he was and continues to be plagued by serious allegations about serious abuse of power; true, he is accused of giving too much space to his wife; true, he has been known to race-bait; true, he is considered a womaniser; and true, his climb to power has been facilitated tremendously by the memory of his illustrious father.

But because he is a career politician; because he is known as a good manager; and because he debonair compared to his predecessor, how he would perform as prime minister was uncertain.

Would he rise to the occasion? Would he rise above his reputation? Though he would not have a honeymoon period as premier the way Abdullah had had, many were hoping that he would reveal some hidden potential.

Indeed, for a man who had seemed destined to be prime minister ever since Anwar Ibrahim was dismissed in September 1998, and whose strategy of staying loyal as deputy to Abdullah in the face of Mahathir's attacks on the latter, these were not exactly the best times for him to come to power.

The opposition is now a force that is formidable in a way Malaysia had not seen since the 1960s; urban voters are, at a time when many young Malays are moving at a fast rate to live among non-Muslim in the cities, demanding better governance; Umno's allies, having been domesticated too thoroughly within the BN stable, are unable to rejuvenate themselves and are waiting for their dominant partner to turn things around; the economy is in crisis at a time when many other Asian countries have become veritable competitors in ways that are hurting Malaysia, especially in attracting foreign direct investments and in providing cheap labour; the budget deficit of 7.4% (for 2009) is the highest since the 1980s.

And above all this, inter-ethnic and inter-religious ties are at a new low.

Six-and-a-half years after Tun Dr Mahathir Mohamad left office – though not the limelight – the reforms that Malaysia needs remain the same. They are basically all institutional. Even where the economy is concerned, the long-term effects of huge wastages through corruption and opaque governance, perpetuated by a conscious policy of intimidation against whistleblowers, journalists, NGO activists and opposition politicians, are now too obvious to be ignored. The intimidation has been handled by Najib's cousin, the Home Affairs Minister Hishammuddin, son of Hussein Onn, Najib's father's successor as prime minister.

In February 2010, the Najib administration's decision to delay parliamentary discussions for the implementation of the Goods and

Services Tax tells an interesting story about the dilemmas facing Najib. Not is he only caught between a rock and a hard place, he has also to decide between the frying pan and the fire.

First, the government presented the GST Bill with the obvious intention of raising money for what many suspect is an empty national coffer. The fact that Najib would present the opposition, which had been reeling in recent months from sustained attacks from all arms of the central government, with an explosive issue that was not racial or religious in character reveals his desperation as Finance Minister.

Second, such a tax would hit indiscriminately at all consumers. It is not a class-conscious measure and will therefore hurt the poor much more than the rich. This would have generated more widespread dissatisfaction than there already is.

Third, in a country where policy-making is race-based and religion-sensitive, implementing a comprehensive tax that affected the Malays as much as the non-Malays would see opportunists within Najib's own party trying to outshine Najib and Umno as champions of the Malay community.

Fourth, GST evasion is a major problem even in the best managed countries in the world. In corruption-riddled Malaysia, where the civil service is suffering a major confidence problem, the process of collecting this tax and minimising evasion will be quite insurmountable.

What all this tells us about Najib's situation today are these; (1) he has to deal with a strong opposition that does represent a stable constituency. So far, his people seem to have chosen to fight through intrigues and intimidation; (2) the income gap in general, between ethnic groups and within ethnic groups remains a serious basic problem that has been ignored for too long. Federal incomes from oil – which has postponed the moment of reckoning for the federal government for decades – are also expected to fall quite soon; (3) Najib's control over Umno is far from certain. As in the case of Abdullah, policies hatched at the centre, and which are not unpopular among party warlords do not get adopted. Overzealousness on that front leads to changes in leadership; (4) the mismanagement of governance that had for decades been legitimized by the awesome and vague goal of righting economic imbalances among races has come home to roost. The deterioration of educational institutions has led to unaccountability and incompetence in the civil service and corruption all round. Reforms, at the same time, have to rely on implementation by the very institutions they seek to change.

One thing that the GST issue does not reflect is how badly recent events have adversely affected Malaysia's reputation in the world. These include the caning of women for illicit sex, the pending caning of a woman for drinking beer, the burning of churches, a demonstration with a distasteful display of a cow's head against the building of the Hindu temple, the formation of an ultra-right Malay group, Perkasa, which was given an immediate publishing licence, the ban on non-Malays to use the word "Allah"; the refusal to allow a book critical of Mahathir Mohamad to be sold in the country; the tragic death of an opposition aide from a fall off the building of the anti-corruption agency; and the trial against opposition leader Anwar Ibrahim on a sodomy rape charge.

The fall in FDI and the increasing brain drain out of the country are undeniable evidence of how badly needed reform of major institutions are to the future well-being of the country.

As long as they are delayed, the decay of Malaysia's many institutions, especially Umno and the BN, continues, as will inter-ethnic tension, economic stagnation, the brain drain, falling standards of education, widespread corruption, and abuse of power and incompetence in the police, the judiciary and the civil service in general.

Malaysia – and the federal government – needs to bite the bullet while some major surgery is carried out. The ailment is terminal, and as far as I can see, there are no anaesthetics available.

OOI KEE BENG
March 2010

THE CHAPTERS

Feeding that addiction*

MALAYSIANS love their by-elections; and as Scandinavians like to say, "a cherished offspring is given many names".

And so, we see how Malaysian by-elections get endlessly analysed, and how their significance gets exaggerated.

This enthrallment with by-elections is quite understandable if we consider how strongly the Barisan Nasional (BN) and the United Malays National Organisation (Umno) had dominated politics, and how politically sensitive information is kept inaccessible.

A pathological thirst for knowledge about political sympathies was bound to develop under such circumstances.

In the days before March 8, 2008, by-elections were interesting mainly for how much they revealed of the BN's reputedly formidable and well-funded electoral apparatus. Instead of looking for shifts in voter support, one looked for the relative efficacy of government manipulation of voters and votes.

After that fateful date, the concern about by-elections is reminiscent of a tsunami watch. No doubt, we are talking about waves on little lakes, and not oceans, since a by-election involves only a restricted group of voters.

But nevertheless, an indicator is an indicator. It points to a certain direction, and so one can always stretch the line to reveal trends.

During the by-election period, every constituency somehow becomes representative of the national electorate.

---

* *First published in Singapore's Today on 10 January 2009.*

Perhaps, this is an unavoidable effect of Mr Abdullah Ahmad Badawi's prolonged retirement from power, but also of his postponed reformation of a stubborn political establishment that suffered — and in many ways still suffers — from hubris. But more definitely, this is the result of the hastened pace of the consumption of political news.

In an age of fast food and fast fortunes (and misfortunes), five years between every general election is simply too long a time to wait. Loving politics as much as they do, and with the Internet exciting their craving for the latest juicy indication of political trends, Malaysians are now hooked on fast politics as well.

The latest by-election, and the sixth since Mr Abdullah became Prime Minister in October 2003, is taking place in Kuala Terengganu on Jan 17.

The first four were easily won by the BN. All happened during his first term in office. The fifth was held after the March 8 general election last year, and on Mr Anwar Ibrahim's home turf of Permatang Pauh. There, the BN lost badly.

Now, barely five months after Permatang Pauh, Malaysians are getting their next attack of ballot fever.

At a time when the state of federal politics remains foggy, the perceived national significance of the Kuala Terengganu by-election is necessarily exaggerated.

First, it is being considered, not as the last by-election of the Abdullah period, but as the first of the Najib Abdul Razak period. This is partially strengthened by the fact that Mr Najib, as Deputy Prime Minister, is commander-in-chief for BN's by-elections, including this one. A loss for BN would be seen as his personal loss.

Second, a BN victory would mean that Mr Najib does enjoy popular Malay support. A BN defeat will thus be taken as a sign that he lacks support outside Umno.

Third, a win for Mr Anwar's opposition — although only one seat is up for grabs — will be taken to mean that the voter revolt against the BN continues steadily. A defeat will not necessarily say the opposite because the parliamentary seat in question has been a BN seat.

Fourth, since the Chinese vote may turn out to be the decisive factor, a loss for BN will be taken as a sign that the Malaysian Chinese

Association (MCA), Umno's main ally, is once again failing to deliver the numbers.

A BN win, on the other hand, will indeed be taken to mean that the MCA is still a force to be reckoned with.

The thing is, someone has to win. That is the nature of the game. And in a case that is too close to call in advance of the campaigning itself, one should not take the result in itself to signify anything definite.

But besides the perceived and exaggerated significance of all the presently imaginable results, there are meatier matters that bear studying about the by-election. All these have to do with the campaign period itself.

How the parties and the coalitions behave and fare in the campaigning period is what is of greater interest. And the mass media, old and new, will be watching and reporting every step and misstep.

A clearer idea about the unity of the Parti Islam SeMalaysia (PAS) and Umno, or the lack of it, and the cohesion of Pakatan Rakyat and the BN, or the lack of it, can be gained when these bodies suffer the strain of campaigning.

The Pakatan tide continues*

ELECTION results cannot help but provide an exhausted citizenry relief from the suspense of the weeks preceding Polling Day. More than that, they are a reality check on the political state of affairs.

That is one reason why polls are so captivating, and when carried out fairly, they also leave all involved on all sides with the feeling that they did take part in something grand and meaningful.

Naturally, a by-election tells much less than what a general election would and the consequences of the results are infinitely less imposing.

That is true for normal times. But these are not normal times in Malaysia.

The Kuala Terengganu by-election on Saturday took place right in the middle of a protracted battle between the ruling Barisan Nasional (BN) and the opposition Pakatan Rakyat (PR) that started even before the latter was properly formed on April 1 last year.

There appears to be no end to this war of wits and the weaving of intrigues. Perhaps that is the point of a democracy — to institutionalise inherent differences and thus, defuse their potential to cause violence.

Buoyed by their success in last year's March 8 elections, and indeed as if in answer to a calling, the Democratic Action Party (DAP), Parti Islam SeMalaysia (PAS) and Parti Keadilan Rakyat (PKR) could not but make one more attempt at forming a coalition that could finally challenge the BN for federal power.

---

* *First published in Singapore's Today on 19 January 2009.*

With PAS' success in Kuala Trengganu, the baby that is the PR has survived its shaky infancy.

BN has now lost two by-elections in a row, and badly at that. The first was when former Deputy Prime Minister Anwar Ibrahim was elected back into Parliament in August last year.

With these coming after the drubbing that the government suffered in the general elections, and if we consider how consistently BN won four by-elections duringMr Abdullah Badawi's first mandate period, it is hard for anyone to continue claiming that the tide has indeed changed for BN.

However, what the PR needs to be cognizant of is exactly the fact that tides do change. No doubt the three member-parties of PR will ride the present gush in their favour for as long as they can. Malaysians can only hope that it will wash away much that has gone wrong with BN and put into place institutions and values that will take the country into a new stage of concerted development.

To steal one of United States President-elect Barack Obama's lines — who does not do that nowadays? — we may be witnessing a rebirth of inter-ethnic cooperation taking place in Malaysia. The first birth took place in the '50s under Tunku Abdul Rahman Putra, and the second happens now, half a century later.

Identifying the differences between the two conceptions and the two births may provide a roadmap for how the new-born consensus is to be nurtured.

Now, when the Islamist party actually won over 3,000 votes more than it did 10 months ago in the Kuala Trengganu parliamentary constituency, its members cannot avoid learning at the nation-wide level that non-Muslims are not necessarily going to vote against it.

If non-Muslims are indeed part of its potential constituency, then there is an understanding that dialogues are necessary.

Pakatan Rakyat's achievement in its nine-month existence is this: Being able to sell the idea to otherwise race-fixated Malaysians that they are not each other's enemies and their battles do not have to be fought by proxy through race-based political parties.

This is not a new product. It was sold once upon a time to Malayans in the twilight years of British domination of Malaya by Tunku Abdul Rahman. But much has changed since then. That was no longer the product that BN had been selling over the last couple of decades.

The most important change is the fact that the country has been ruled for 50 years by an increasingly powerful BN that grew more corrupt, more callous, more uncaring and less incompetent. It had become a goal unto itself.

With hubris eating up BN credibility and the population hollowed of hope, the tide turned and a rebirth of inter-ethnic cooperation became necessary.

"Enough is enough" is thus the common sentiment through which the two conceptions took place. As in March last year, Chinese and Indians voted in Kuala Trengganu for a Malay-based party outside BN's framework.

That had been BN's trump card. It has now lost that monopoly. Tides ebb and babies age. BN waited too long to reinvent itself.

Nations live on a diet of successive myths. Once one is gone, another is adopted. The latest myths to go are that Malaysia's fate is synonymous with BN's fate, and the well-being of the Malay community is dependent on the well-being of the once-dominant United Malays National Organisation.

The painful path towards devolution*

THE transformation in Malaysian politics that started with the March 8 general elections left the opposition with control over five states in the north, and robbed the ruling Barisan Nasional (BN) of its traditional 2/3 majority in parliament.

Three patterns were made manifest in the process. First, the greatest changes occurred at the state level; second, a geographical divide became undeniable; and third, all the allies of the dominant United Malays National Organisation (Umno) on the northern half of the peninsula suffered much greater relative losses than that party did at the state level.

But with Anwar Ibrahim, the opposition leader, trying so hard to topple the central government over the last few months and with two by-elections won by the opposition being parliamentary – and not state – affairs, the real dimensions at which political transformation was taking place was forgotten.

The country's focus became fixed, firstly on Anwar's Pakatan Rakyat (PR) trying to transcend the 50% limit in parliament, and secondly on whether PR can win the Sarawak state elections due by 2011.

What the electoral success of the disparate parties within the PR strongly suggested was that different states were favouring different parties to represent them. This is a clear reflection and recognition of the cultural and geographical diversity of the country.

---

* First published in Opinion Asia.com on 11 February 2009.

One main reason why Malaysia had failed in homogenising its population along lines of education, culture and language was because this diversity was badly underestimated. In the early years, the central government, under security threats from Indonesia and the Philippines, as well as domestic communists, grew much stronger in all ways than the original federalist format of the country had proposed.

The March 8 electoral results amounted to a bold attempt from below, starting in the northern parts of the peninsula, at loosening federal authoritarianism, and in curbing its many excesses.

In the five PR states taken as a whole, the Malaysian Chinese Association lost 87% of its representation; the Parti Gerakan Rakyat Malaysia lost 84% and the Malaysian Indian Congress ended up with no representation at all after losing all its four state seats. Umno did surprisingly well, relatively speaking, losing no more than 39% of its state seats.

The BN as a whole thus retreated by 57% in the northern states, excepting Perlis.

The five states, in this context, bear studying individually. We see that the BN holds only 20 of 56 seats in Selangor. More significantly, Umno's allies hold only two such seats there, down from 19 in 2004. These hold none of the 55 state seats in Kelantan (with Umno holding 6), none of the 40 in Penang (with Umno holding 11), control two of 36 in Kedah (with Umno holding 12), and one of 59 in Perak (with Umno holding 28 before the crossovers earlier this week).

What these figures show are, firstly, that Umno's allies have become shockingly irrelevant in the north, and, secondly, that the frontlines of the continuous battle between the BN (read Umno in this case) and the PR cut through Kedah where the PR has a six-seat majority, Negri Sembilan in the south where the BN control has an equally narrow advantage, and most dramatically, through Perak, where the BN now claims to have realised enough crossovers to fell the PR government under Mentri Besar Nizar Jamaluddin.

Besides these fault lines on the peninsula, one must also consider the volatile situation in the East Malaysian states of Sabah and Sarawak, where sounds of discontent grow louder by the day. Not only will the BN's hold on power be seriously challenged there, but with the diverse ethnic quality of these states becoming more and more relevant, the definite ethnic categorisations so vital to BN politics risk being undermined.

In Perak, the situation will continue to be unstable for a while since that state, as far as the electoral results are concerned, is the major frontline for the battle between the old and the new. This battle goes beyond a simple choice between two coalitions, and is in reality part of the historical process of federal devolution that the diversity of the various parts of the country requires in the long run.

The larger picture – given how the BN structure has lost relevance in the north – is that although the fortunes of war may sway now one way, then the other, the demand for a better representation of the country's diversity will continue to be raised.

04

Advantage Najib? BN may pay a high price for Perak polarisation*

THE change in government in the Malaysian state of Perak carries with it great implications for a long list of actors on both sides.

The Pakatan Rakyat (PR) government of Mr Mohd Nizar Jamaluddin has been replaced by the Barisan Nasional (BN) coalition following controversial defections that left the state assembly with 28 on each side, and with three independents declaring support for the BN.

There has definitely been a shift in power and a realignment of forces has certainly taken place. However, what we are witnessing is far from being an end game of any kind. The game goes on. Indeed, it is not even clear who the real winners actually are. A lot depends on the time frame one chooses to use.

In the short term, Premier-in-waiting Najib Abdul Razak certainly did gain an advantage — he did manage to outsmart the Pakatan Rakyat state government. He displayed to the United Malays National Organisation (Umno) that he does have leadership qualities, and that he has able advisers.

The Perak crisis undoubtedly improved Mr Najib's stature just in time for the Umno elections next month, when he is to become party president, and therefore Prime Minister of the country.

But since his claim to the presidency is in no doubt, the practical advantage of his success in felling the PR government in Perak lies

---

* *First published in Singapore's Today on 14 February 2009.*

more in bolstering support for candidates he favours for other positions in the party than anything else.

One other person keeping an eye on the party elections is Mr Khairy Jamaluddin, the son-in-law of Prime Minister Abdullah Ahmad Badawi. Mr Khairy is one of the three candidates trying to become the head of Umno Youth. After the trouncing that Umno received in last year's general elections, Mr Khairy had been trying to reinvent himself as a closet liberal on the verge of coming out.

Mr Khairy grasped the opportunity offered by the Perak crisis to defend a purported challenge to the Perak royal house, and called for Mr Nizar to be expelled from Perak. This return to hardline methods undid much of the hard work Mr Khairy had been putting into improving his image in the eyes of the general public.

PR's anger at losing a government caused leading members of the coalition such as Mr Nizar and Mr Karpal Singh, a Member of Parliament and a veteran of the Democratic Action Party (DAP), to express dissatisfaction at Sultan Azlan Shah. Mr Karpal went so far as to threaten to sue the monarch.

The popularity that the Perak sovereign had enjoyed before the crisis dropped sharply after he refused to dissolve the state assembly at Mr Nizar's request but instead granted the BN — which lost the state in last year's elections — the right to build a new government based on support from PR defectors.

The outraged Mr Karpal had also called for opposition leader Anwar Ibrahim to take responsibility for PR's defeat and resign. DAP's secretary-general Lim Guan Eng had immediately reprimanded Mr Karpal and advised him to use internal channels for expressing his dissatisfaction. Mr Karpal is under pressure from all sides to retrace his steps.

High price of victory

Mr Anwar is being given much of the blame for the crisis, seeing how he was the one who had, since March 8 last year, been attempting to engineer defections from the BN in order to gain federal power. Pressure on him to regain the initiative in the ongoing battle with Mr Najib is also mounting. Two upcoming by-elections will provide Mr Anwar with that chance.

In the long run though, the victors may have to pay a high price for the Perak "coup".

What the four defectors in this Shakespearean drama will actually gain is not clear in any way. Aside from whatever might have been promised them by the BN, their political future looks very bleak indeed.

The two PR-defecting assemblymen were, and are, facing corruption charges. The BN offer for them to switch sides promised them some respite. But as with Mr Nasaruddin Hashim, the BN defector who triggered the drama on Jan 26 and who re-defected 10 days later, the duo cannot expect a long career in politics.

DAP's Hee Jit Foong's decision to fell the government — whether done for monetary gains, for position or to spite her party — has made her a hated person in her constituency, and it is a mystery how she imagines to continue being in the public eye after her defection.

The lesson that the PR has to learn from this is that it cannot hope to achieve stable and good governance in the long run if incompetence and a lack of commitment continue to riddle its ranks. Many of its state assemblymen gained positions beyond their ability to manage following the March 8 voter revolt. The PR will have to take on the uncomfortable task of dismissing inept loyalists and replacing them with new talents in some graceful fashion.

It will also have to imagine a life after Mr Anwar. To do that, it has to form coalitional institutions to keep dialogue and understanding alive among its members.

As for the BN, the price that it will have to pay will not be small. Further polarisation has now taken place, not least among Perakians, and much anger has been stirred up against Mr Najib's methods. This will make it practically impossible for non-Malay BN parties in the north to campaign in any effective fashion in coming elections.

The Perak crisis also reminds Malaysians that the war between the coalitions will continue for a long time to come, and where the peninsula is concerned, it will be fought in the electoral frontline states of not only Perak, but also Kedah and Negri Sembilan.

05

A cyber war in Malaysian politics?*

ONCE upon a time, before the Internet became as common as the television in Malaysian homes, public figures made local speeches that were tailored to suit the audience that was physically present.

This worked well for politicians wishing to entertain the parochial tendencies of the audience of the day without jeopardising their prospects of becoming nationally relevant.

Today, however, such speeches quickly leak into the wired world of the Internet, putting things into a different context, and revealing the speakers' supposed real values to the world.

Playing local politics with the awareness that the audience is always the whole wide world is no easy task, especially for those who have been in politics and in power long before the Internet changed everything.

The dominant Umno learned this the hard way three years ago when it decided to telecast "live" its national assembly. The parochialism and racism expressed by its candidates on that occasion for the nation to hear soon forced it to backtrack.

Defensive arrogance does grow out of the inability to evolve.

The attempt to block access to Raja Petra Kamarudin's controversial Malaysia Today website last year managed to stop traffic going to that site, but did not stop access to its contents. Mirror sites sprung up immediately to nullify the censorship.

---

* *First published in Singapore's Today on 19 February 2009.*

The police decision in September 2008 to use the Internal Security Act to jail Raja Petra, along with prominent opposition politician Teresa Kok and journalist Tan Hoon Cheng, merely backfired. The de facto minister of law, Datuk Zaid Ibrahim, soon resigned in protest.

Publicly calling female bloggers liars, as then Tourism Minister Tengku Adnan Tengku Mansor did in March 2007, is also not a very smart thing to do. The negative reaction on the web on that occasion was tremendous.

Opinions expressed for local consumption becoming national news is part and parcel of a revolution in information technology which carries enormous consequences for the near future. Some are positive, and some will certainly not be.

Through the Net, you can sell old useless books you have under the stairs on the world market; you can get to know strangers on the other half of the world merely by being on chat sites; and you can arrange an entire holiday to the south of France without talking to any salesperson at all.

In Malaysian politics, we have witnessed how SMSes, videos and phone cameras have come into play. While these can uncover abuse of power, as in the case of the woman forced to do ear-squats naked while detained by the police in December 2005; reveal dubious practices, as in the case of the Lingam Tapes released in 2007 showing a prominent lawyer boasting about his ability to fix top judge appointments through political connections; and contribute to court cases, as in SMSes supposedly sent by Deputy Prime Minister Datuk Seri Najib Razak to a lawyer, discussing the detention of a close associate then charged with involvement in the murder of a Mongolian woman.

The latest political incident involving IT innovations concerns the circulation of nude pictures of prominent opposition politician Elizabeth Wong, secretly taken on a phone camera.

The case of Wong (also a blogger), who has offered to resign from her position as state assemblywoman for the opposition-held Selangor, adds worrying dimensions to the political use of modern IT.

First, it is not only the line between the local and the national that is being erased. The line between the private and the public is fading fast as well.

That is worrying indeed. Most urbanites in Malaysia of all races, especially in the Klang Valley where Wong lives, would undoubtedly consider Wong the victim. Mass media attempts to class the case as a "sex scandal" — and this happened on both sides of the Causeway — smack of shameless sensationalism, journalistic amateurism and political opportunism.

In the sanctity of her home, surely she is allowed to walk scantily dressed, sleep half-naked, even shower nude, and yes, have sex without clothes on. The culprits deserving punishment are those who facilitated the publicising of those pictures, regardless of whether they were taken with her permission or not.

The fact that she is an unmarried woman, and not a man, has had a serious impact on how the incident is being interpreted. Should a male politician, married or not, such as former Selangor Menteri Besar Datuk Seri Dr Khir Toyo, for example, have been photographed in the nude while asleep, the fallout would have been minimal, even comical.

The Wong case also shows the disturbing shrinkage of moral space when the private and the local are technologically subsumed under the public and the national.

Moral values do differ geographically, individually, culturally and according to lifestyle. This diversity is denied when such a case gets politicised, and here, the supposed sensitivities of the vocally most religious, most parochial, most traditional and most rural are allowed to define the national public norm. Wong is being sacrificed to appease illiberal elements within the opposition. Surely, this is not what the Pakatan Rakyat is fighting for.

A political cyber war has started in Malaysia. While we thought that the old would be at the mercy of the new in such a showdown, it is time to realise that, in truth, the more desperate and more immoral has the edge.

06

Bewildered in Malaysia, perplexed in Perak, stupefied in Selangor*

THE energy fuelling the electoral tsunami that saw members of the opposition coalition Pakatan Rakyat (PR) win in five states in northern Malaysia last March was general indignation over the rapidly deteriorating state of governance in the country.

With the ruling coalition, the Barisan Nasional (BN), still not showing signs of reforming itself a year down the road, this indignation is turning into bewilderment.

The coup-through-defections against the PR government of Perak is still being played out, with the Sultan's decision to hand over power to the BN being challenged with full force.

The PR Chief Minister Mohd Nizar Jamaluddin has taken his successor as Chief Minister, Mr Zambry Abdul Kadir, to court for usurping his position, while the Speaker of the State Assembly, Mr V Sivakumar, has suspended Mr Zambry for 18 months from the legislature for contempt, and his five exco appointees for a year.

These latest moves are designed to force Sultan Azlan Shah to concede that all parties will have to return to the Perak electorate for the final say. The fear is that musclemen may be moved in to solve the constitutional crisis.

One further incident that is worrying the general public is the spreading of semi-nude photos of opposition leader Elizabeth Wong. These had been taken on the sly, apparently by an ex-boyfriend with his camera phone while she was asleep in her apartment.

---

* *First published in Singapore's Today on 21 February 2009.*

Outraged, saddened and feeling violated, this prominent assemblywoman of Selangor state has offered to resign. There was pressure on her to act in order to pre-empt a split in the PR, if and when certain Islamists may feel forced to criticise her for moral reasons. The coalition will decide her fate next week.

The vocal segment of the Malaysian public is expressing outrage over the fact that the apparent victim of a crime is being punished. This follows three lines of reasoning.

Firstly, had Ms Wong been a man whose semi-nude pictures, taken without his consent, were distributed to the mass media, political repercussions would have been minimal.

Secondly, the invasion of privacy in this case was so blatant the mass media should not have tried to capitalise on it, and politicians such as former Selangor Chief Minister Khir Toyo, a BN leader badly tainted by allegations of wrongdoings, should not be calling for her immediate resignation.

Thirdly, the country's ethical diversity is being denied to the extent that the supposed sensitivities of those most willing to demand ethical conformity of others are being given decisive and undue consideration.

While no link to the BN has been identified where the Elizabeth Wong case is concerned, most fingers are definitely pointing at elements in the government as the parties guilty of facilitating the release of the pictures.

Opposition parliamentarian Jeff Ooi has gone so far as to suggest on his popular website that Ms Wong's ex-boyfriend, Mr Malek Hilmi, was one of several "Trojan horses" placed within the PR camp as aides in the confusion following PR's surprise victories in last year's general elections. Another such "horse", claims Mr Ooi, was Mr Mohd Saiful Bukhari Azlan, Mr Anwar Ibrahim's aide who has levelled charges of sodomy rape against his former boss.

Mr Anwar himself has also accused the BN for being behind the release of Ms Wong's pictures.

Premier-in-waiting Najib Abdul Razak has denied any BN connection to the case, and is challenging PR leaders to substantiate their claims. In the event, Mr Najib failed to take moral advantage of the situation to act as the Premier-in-waiting and take a decided stand against the political misuse of Ms Wong's ordeal by BN leaders such as Mr Khir.

A state of disbelief

In truth, the political game in Malaysia has reached the level where intrigues and hidden tactics are the order of the day, where the mass media, the police and the judiciary are no longer expected to act professionally, objectively, and with integrity.

Politicians, even leading politicians, are certainly not expected to act like statesmen, and in a non-partisan manner.

Under such circumstances, no one really expects any proof to be reliable or made readily available. Indeed, proof becomes rather superfluous where faith and trust in the institutions of state are in short supply.

Perception is everything in politics, and in Malaysia, where the BN has been in power since independence and controls — and has consequently compromised — all the institutions of government to varying degrees, any episode that hurts the opposition is invariably believed to bear BN's fingerprints.

No evidence either way, be it in the Perak crisis or the Wong case, or even in the many politically charged criminal cases being heard at the moment in Malaysian courts, is taken at face value by the public.

Malaysia's addiction to conspiracy theories is quite incurable, fed as it is by dose after dose of bewildering episodes and partisan posturing.

It is not only Perak that is suffering a constitutional crisis. The whole country is mired in a misguided democracy.

07

Still suffering from growing pains[*]

THERE are basically two related ways of understanding the year that has been since March 8, 2008.

One is to recognise the many dramatic events of the past 12 months as part and parcel of an accelerating upheaval which is seeing the monolithic structure of Malaysia's Barisan Nasional (BN) being replaced by a two-coalition system.

This turmoil challenges in concrete terms not only the symbiosis between ethnicity and political party, but also the balance of power, both between the federal government and the state governments, as well as between elected representatives and the aristocracy.

The second way is to view the past year as a litmus test for Malaysian democracy, through which its level of maturity can be ascertained.

Of course, the very fact that the upheaval mentioned above is taking place at all tells us that Malaysian democracy is at an impasse caused by nothing less than a decisive swing in voter sentiment throughout the northern states.

This sudden political engagement in itself tells us that Malaysia's democracy is still suffering growing pains. It is far from mature and some would say that its growth is badly stunted, but it is nevertheless not frozen in time.

---

[*]   *First published in Singapore's Today on 7 March 2009.*

More and more showdowns between the two coalitions are to be expected in the coming months, most of which will be of a constitutional nature.

Democratic maturity is best observed in a number of ways, the most telling of which is how well those who are losing power live with that fact. Here, Malaysia has definitely shown that it has matured beyond the days of May 13, 1969. Angry and disappointed voices had to be expected, but no violence followed the BN's defeats in the north. Voters on both the winning and losing sides are acting in much more civilised ways than before.

Democratic maturity

However, recent events in Perak show that the federal government is not above employing the grey margins of the Constitution to undermine and topple a popularly-elected state government that is not to its liking. BN's ability to accept defeat is therefore not as could be expected in a mature democracy.

The political space now available to the aristocracy reflects the inability of the two camps to play by democratic rules.

The sodomy charge against opposition leader Anwar Ibrahim is seen by many as another case of politically motivated use of the law.

Another salient point to ponder is to what extent leaders of those parties that suffered substantial defeats were willing to take the blame for the results. No leader of any BN component party offered to resign immediately after March 8.

Changes since then have been most thorough in the Malaysian Chinese Association, following its party elections in October last year, with Mr Ong Ka Ting resigning as president. At the same time, Gerakan's leader, Dr Koh Tsu Koon, became party president that same month despite also having led his party to dismal results.

Malaysian Indian Congress president Sami Vellu, who has been the leader most personally blamed for party defeats, seems certain to try to retain his position on April 12, when the party holds its elections.

The United Malays National Organisation (Umno), the dominant factor in the BN, had earlier postponed its party elections until

December last year. After the general elections, it chose to postpone them a further three months.

Its president, Prime Minister Abdullah Badawi, agreed to resign by the end of this month only after intense pressure was put on him by the party's supreme council.

The maturity of most other actors in Malaysia's democratic game is also in doubt. While the federal government has been accused of punishing states that dared vote against it, the many arms of the centrally-salaried civil service have shown a strong prejudice against the opposition-held state governments.

This has been most evident during the Perak constitutional crisis, when the police preferred to obey the State Assembly Secretary in locking out his boss the Speaker — a member of the Pakatan Rakyat (PR) — from the assembly.

The new governments in the PR states, given their goal of reforming governance, have not done too badly, especially if one considers the hurdles they have had to face.

Personnel incompetence at various levels has dogged these governments. However, the personal popularity of new Chief Ministers such as Penang's Lim Guan Eng and Perak's Nizar Jamaluddin increased impressively over the last year.

At the same time, Mr Anwar's ill-advised attempt to topple the federal government through defections must be classed as democratic immaturity on the part of the parliamentary opposition.

But perhaps the clearest signs of maturity are found in voter behaviour. Despite the uncertainties affecting the country and the spate of by-elections since March 8, the Malaysian voter has behaved in an exemplary manner, and has continued to exercise his right to make his voice heard.

This empowerment occurs in tandem with the steady rise in magazine publications, citizen journalism and political blogging. The coming by-elections throughout the country cannot but feed this new fad even further.

Umno's elections are as important as ever[*]

THE End Game has started for what had until recently always been the most significant polls in Malaysia – the party elections of the dominant United Malays National Organization (Umno).

Quite a few special factors come into play in this year's polling,to make it one of the most significant in the party's 63-year-old history, nevertheless.

First, the party president, Prime Minister Abdullah Badawi is stepping down, after having bowed to pressure from the supreme council to take the blame for the battering the party took at the general elections on March 8 last year.

This leaves the field clear for his deputy Najib Abdul Razak to take over as party president and prime minister come April 3, barring any mishap.

Needless to say, this sidelining of Abdullah Badawi, who is well-liked by his followers, has upset many within the party. At the same time, doubts are being freely voiced about Najib's unsuitability for the job, given his lack of contact with common folk and the many allegations made against him, for bad judgement and worse.

Second, these party elections had been postponed twice. It was due in 2007 but was put off for the suspected reason of avoiding party infighting before the snap elections expected in 2008. After the drubbing suffered by the party and its allies in the elections, it was again postponed, this time to March 2009, purportedly to allow Abdullah some time to tie up his administration's loose ends.

---

* *First published in Singapore's Today on 14 March 2009.*

Third, many party members are hoping against hope that by some sleight of hand, history will throw up a leadership that will actually manage to reform the party and save the coalition, slow the ascendance of the opposition and reverse the deteriorating state of governance in the country.

This year, the deputy presidency is being contested, but most observers do not consider any of the candidates for that position or for the supreme council for that matter, to have the will and the clout to do the spring cleaning required.

Perhaps as always, change has to come from among the young. But none of the three candidates vying for the leadership of the influential Youth wing commands the credibility that is required to champion that Herculean task.

Youth deputy head Khairy Jamaluddin, the son-in-law of Abdullah Badawi, who saw his hopes of being in Cabinet smashed by the results of the general elections and by Abdullah's resignation, is aiming to climb one important step up the party hierarchy. His weakness at the moment is the fall of his father-in-law, and he is silently blamed for much that had gone wrong.

The second candidate, Mukhriz Mahathir, is a relative newcomer to the game despite being the son of the former prime minister. He is seen to be lacking the political experience to turn things around, and to be too nice a guy to survive in the long run should he decide to make trouble.

The former Mentri Besar of Selangor state, Khir Toyo, is the third candidate for the position of Youth head. He is spattered with allegations of wrongdoings, and while that had not stopped Umno candidates in getting votes before, the national spirit of the times, especially in the young, does work against tainted politicians.

Khir has started making claims that he is being sabotaged by his opponents, signalling that these Umno elections are not going to be any cleaner than before. Although he did not give details, his worries may be a reaction to accusations being made in the Selangor state assembly about dubious practices carried out during his watch, in some cases involving his wife.

A further indication that the battle for Umno positions will be a many-faceted one is the raid carried out this week by the newly formed

Malaysian Anti-Corruption Commission (MACC) on Tourism Minister Azalina Othman. The minister's political secretary was detained last week with RM75,000 in his car. The suspicion is that the money was for the buying of votes.

Azalina is a candidate for the party supreme council.

This happens at the same time as incumbent supreme councillor Norza Zakaria, who is aiming to retain his position, is being implicated in investigations into vote-buying within the party.

The fight for the leadership of the Women's Wing will be no less exciting. There, old-hand Rafidah Aziz, the former Minister of International Trade and Industry, is riled up at being challenged by her deputy Shahrizat Abdul Jalil, until recently the Minister for Women, Family and Community Development.

This challenge came despite Rafidah's somewhat strange promise to retire in June this year, three months after the party polls.

Shahrizat lost her parliamentary seat in the general elections but was however appointed Special Adviser to the Prime Minister for Women and Social Development Affairs by Abdullah. Rafidah, who did retain her parliamentary seat, was left out of the Cabinet.

Despite Umno's falling fortunes, there is no doubt that the leaders whom the party's divisions choose at the end of this month will continue to influence Malaysian politics for some time to come.

Sad to say, even to an optimist, the chances of them putting the country's well-being before that of party and self are meagre.

09

Can Najib be the reformist Abdullah failed to be?*

FIVE years after the 2004 general elections gave unprecedented support to Mr Abdullah Badawi, he leaves office a disappointed man eased out by his party's leadership.

He also leaves behind a disappointed population that hoped he would reverse the downward trend of governance in Malaysia. He also hands over office to a man who, unlike him, will start his term under tremendous pressure to perform.

Mr Najib Abdul Razak, the eldest son of the country's second Prime Minister, will, barring any last minute move by his political enemies, become the sixth Prime Minister of the country. This is a role he — and his wife — seem to think is destined for him to play.

In fact, he will be holding not one, but three if not four, pivotal positions at the same time. According to tradition, the country's Prime Minister is also the president of the United Malays National Organisation (Umno) as well as the chairman of the ruling coalition, the Barisan Nasional (BN).

Chances are, he will take on at least one other major portfolio. He became Finance Minister only recently and will therefore probably continue to be such. The Home Ministry is one further administration that he might be tempted to control directly.

---

* *First published in Singapore's Today on 28 March 2009.*

The immediate challenges Mr Najib will face as Prime Minister radiate from this triple pyramidal system of government that Malaysia has always had.

Forming a Cabinet that will bring the "massive change" that he recently promised Malaysians is his first Herculean task. His first picks have to come from among Umno's leaders. He will have to accommodate newly-elected leaders of the various wings of the party as well as from among the supreme councillors.

In doing this, he has to balance the various factions within the party. Alienating any of them badly will increase chances of defections to the opposition further down the road.

Umno's biggest problem at the moment is its inability to win support from among young Malays. It is losing urban areas to Parti Keadilan Rakyat and the rural north to Parti Islam SeMalaysia.

Corruption is seen to have corroded the party at all levels and many suspect that the only way it can reinvent itself is to lose power, just as the Kuomintang in Taiwan had to do.

After making hard choices from among Umno's leaders, Mr Najib has to, in keeping with the BN's claim to represent all major ethnic groups, place prominent non-Malay allies in middle-rank portfolios.

Given how parties such as Parti Gerakan Rakyat and the Malaysian Indian Congress (MIC) were decimated in last year's general elections, their leaders who had lost their Parliamentary seats will have to be made senators first before they can constitutionally become Cabinet Ministers. Doing this repeatedly will inevitably be taken as a snub by voters.

Not giving high positions to leaders such as Gerakan's Koh Tsu Koon and MIC's Samy Vellu will, however, almost definitely estrange them and their supporters.

BN's biggest problem at the moment is its inability to regain the Indian vote, and the uncontested re-election as MIC president of Mr Samy Vellu, the man blamed for alienating the Indian community, undermines the raison d'etre of the coalition further.

Constrained by the power balance of his party and of the damaged coalition that he leads, Mr Najib, at the personal level, has no choice but to seek the moral high ground. This will take some doing, seeing how the murder trial of the Mongolian woman, Ms Altantuya Shaaribuu, continues to haunt him.

All the new Prime Minister can do is to hope that the affair will fade away from public consciousness after the court's verdict is handed out next month. "Revelations" about his connection or lack of connection, to the sordid case is no longer an option for him.

Instead, Mr Najib will have to drown himself in the work of softening the worst effects of the emerging economic crisis.

Serious dialogue with civil society — if not with the opposition parties — is a tactic he has to adopt, not for its own sake, but because that is the only way for him to project himself as a Prime Minister for the country, not for party or coalition. That is also the only chance he has to slow the flow of voter support away from the BN.

Relying only on Umno and the BN merely strengthens the image of insularity and arrogance that voters punished the government for last year.

The optimism and pro-activeness that Mr Najib needs to project depends on his ability to keep his three major roles apart. He has to persuade Malaysians that he is the nation's leader, first and foremost, and not the defender of his party's and his coalition's vested interests.

His political future depends on him acting tough against his own. Radical reforms from the top are the only answer.

10

What Najib needs*

AND so, after holding the sceptre of power for five and a half years, Datuk Seri Abdullah Ahmad Badawi now passes it to Datuk Seri Najib Razak.

While Abdullah's ascendance to power in 2003 was greeted with cheers from Malaysians, his retirement is being met with grave apprehension. This is not because his term in office was an exciting one. Rather, it is because the weakened state of Umno and the ruling Barisan Nasional (BN) is further aggravated by the low esteem in which Najib is being held.

Nevertheless, given how so many within Umno, including Najib himself, seem to buy into the idea that the eldest son of the second premier, Tun Abdul Razak Hussein, is fated to be Malaysia's leader, nothing has been able to stop Najib's climb to the top.

But staying there will not be an easy business.

For one thing, there is no status quo that Najib can rest upon. He takes over the ship in the middle of a storm — a tsunami, if I may be allowed to use the tired imagery one more time — and so, his new administration has to move fast, and be seen to move fast, in one direction or another.

Making promises and then taking one's time to fulfill them in watered-down form did not work for Abdullah, and for certain will not work for Najib.

---

* *First published in Malaysia's The Nutgraph on 1 April 2009.*

Adopting Tun Dr Mahathir Mohamad's authoritarianism is not possible either, basically because Najib is not Mahathir; Umno and the BN have never been as weak as they are now; and Malaysians today — post-8 March — are not what they were a couple of decades ago.

The times are a-changing, and the more things change, the less they stay the same.

Wanted: New discourse

The crisis of confidence that Umno and its allies are suffering from is due to them ignoring a basic rule in nation building: the words of leaders must actually carry real meaning to a representative cross-section of the population. These words must touch people, excite them and give them hope.

A national discourse that expresses the gravity, integrity and sincerity of the government is vital to a country's stability. Otherwise, why pay attention to a government that either threatens you, takes you for a fool, or embarrasses you?

Umno's problem is that it allowed its own internal discourse to become the national discourse. The party's excessive concerns about losing the religious vote made it lose both the non-religious and religious vote. Its outmoded rhetoric made it lose the vote of young Malaysians of all races. Its fixation with Malay dominance made it lose the non-Malay Malaysian vote. And its desire to make the party increasingly dominant made its allies weak and its enemies strong.

Historically, Umno did manage to conduct discourses that captured general attention and gained it the right to rule the country.

In the 1950s, the twin goals of gaining independence and fighting the communists led to inspired innovations such as the Alliance model and the so-called social contract between Umno and its coalitional allies.

The 1960s was a difficult period when the Malaysia project almost collapsed and the Indonesians posed a serious threat to the country. The riots of 1969 showed that Umno and the Alliance — the precursor to the BN — failed to rejuvenate the national discourse to deal with new socioeconomic challenges.

Radical reforms carried out since 1970 to transform the colonial economy into one more suitable for a multiracial nation state did bring stable growth. Although this was done at the price of muffling parliament and the public, there was sufficient support for the New Economic Policy (NEP) goals of diminishing economic disparities and professional differentiations between the major ethnic groups.

When the NEP officially ended in 1990, Mahathir managed to initiate the ideas of Vision 2020 and Bangsa Malaysia. This allowed Malaysians to hope for the best in the near future while tolerating current discomforts.

With the 1997-98 crisis, Malaysia entered a new era. The Datuk Seri Anwar Ibrahim trials and the Reformasi movement split the country fundamentally. This was seen clearly in the 1999 general election results.

When Abdullah took over in 2003, his promise of institutional reforms functioned in lieu of a proper national discourse, and managed to unite the country for a while.

Once it was clear that his reform agenda had failed, Malaysia's lack of a uniting discourse once again became apparent.

Now when Abdullah leaves the stage a disappointed man and Najib takes over, it is vital that the new leader tries to create a discourse that is inclusive rather than exclusive.

Should Najib fail to do that, he can be sure that the opposition will do its best to step right in.

11

Najib now has to deliver on his promises[*]

BRAND-NEW Prime Minister Datuk Seri Najib Abdul Razak is not in an enviable position.

While some fear that he will try to be a second Tun Dr Mahathir Mohamad who will force party, Parliament and opposition to toe his line, chances are great that he will instead be a second Datuk Seri Abdullah Ahmad Badawi.

For one thing, Najib lacks the conviction and the self-confidence that Dr Mahathir had. Even if he chooses to show that he can be as Machiavellian as the next man, he has to convince a sufficiently large portion of the masses that the harsh measures he carries out are absolutely necessary. That will not be easy to do.

Secondly, given how little room Najib's allies within the Barisan Nasional have to manoeuvre in, such a choice of direction would practically kill them off. What he really needs to do is to give BN component parties like the MIC, the Parti Gerakan Rakyat and the MCA goodies that their leaders can present to their potential constituencies.

Playing "tough guy" will instead work against allies trying hard to win back voters who deserted them because they compromised too much and allowed their party profiles to be subsumed under the federal government's Umno-centrism.

---

*   *First published in* The Malaysian Insider *on 3 April 2009.*

Championing Malay ethnocentrism too loudly will not help Najib also because the emergent opposition coalition is now largely led by Malays as well. What is worse news for him on this front is that the Muslim card that Dr Mahathir used to good effect in the 1980s is not his to play. No Malay sees Najib as a religious leader in any credible sense.

Even when led by Abdullah, a man with respected religious credentials, Umno failed to gain ground among Muslims. The party led by Najib is definitely not able to adopt a position as champion of Malay Islam.

While BN and Umno had been using variations on their "Malay First" policy to justify most of their actions over a long period of time, their moral failings and the falling standards of governance had been supplying oppositional forces with endless possibilities — and time — to formulate ideas that find an easy response among voters of all ages and ethnic groups.

From this grew the opposition's present impressive ability to repulse most of what the powerful central government can throw at it.

The strange coalition forged between the DAP, Parti Keadilan Rakyat and PAS, weak because of its apparent unholy mix, paradoxically enjoys the advantage, at least as long as they remain in opposition, of having collected most expressions of discontent against the BN government under its umbrella.

Najib's biggest problem as he takes over from a disgraced Abdullah is that the opposition has a great discursive advantage over whatever his administration can think up. Datuk Seri Anwar Ibrahim and his allies keep focusing on governance issues, and call for more transparency, more accountability and more competence in government and the civil service. They talk about helping the needy independent of race, of welfare for the poor, of more freedom of expression, and of amending the affirmative action programme that favours Malays. All these find a ready audience.

Indeed, even the spiritual leader of PAS, Datuk Nik Aziz Nik Mat, has most recently declared his uneasiness over the term "Bumiputera", saying that it smacked of racism.

What makes it less prudent for Najib to use harsh methods against his critics is that his personal reputation is badly injured by public association with the murder of the Mongolian national Altantuya Shaariibuu. Any future unwarranted use of draconian methods that can be directly linked to him will damage his image beyond redemption, if it is not that already.

What Najib would be well-advised to do at this stage, and given how the tide continues moving against him, is to do a repeat of the early Abdullah period, but with a desperate effort at ending with a different punch line.

Najib does seem to be in the promising stage at the moment. He wants Umno's electoral structure reformed, somewhat in the way Dr Mahathir's major opponent, Tengku Razaleigh Hamzah, had been calling for. He is also saying that Malaysia's future development depends on ethnic fissures diminishing, something that most Malaysians would not disagree with, having said it themselves for so long.

But beyond parroting the calls for reforms first voiced by others, Najib has to deliver on his promises, and quickly. In that undertaking, the opposition will not be his main enemies. Umno's warlords and power holders in the present enormous federal bureaucracies will be the ones he will have to combat. He might not have the ability to manage that.

The area where he can concentrate his efforts at showing leadership qualities is in national economic policy-making. With the global crisis getting worse by the day, he is offered the opportunity of being the prime minister who is able to soften its worst effects. Should he manage that, and in the process place the country in an improved international position when and if the next economic boom comes, then he will be able to leave a legacy far more excellent than any Malaysian anywhere in the world expects of him.

12

No let-up in voter revolt[*]

THE results of the triple by-elections that the Election Commission took so much trouble to put on the same day, and a weekday at that, and suitably after the dominant United Malays National Organisation (Umno) had held what was expected to be a disruptive party election, failed to convince Malaysians that the winds of change were now blowing against the opposition.

The Batang Ai state seat in Sarawak was closely watched for signs of whether Parti Keadilan Rakyat (PKR) leader Anwar Ibrahim and his allies had made any headway in persuading East Malaysians to consider an alternative to the Barisan Nasional (BN) government. The increased margin that the BN attained seems to suggest that he has not made any impression, at least among the hill Ibans.

The battle for votes in Sarawak is a protracted one and the Batang Ai by-election has to be seen as a skirmish won by the defending forces.

The by-elections in Kedah and Perak, on the other hand, carries more immediate import, as these states constitute the frontline for the proverbial shooting war between BN and the three-party Pakatan Rakyat (PR) coalition.

Where Bukit Selambau is concerned, there was fear among PR supporters that the Indian vote might be split to the opposition's disadvantage and that the record number of contestants – 13 – might tip the balance in BN's favour, as had traditionally been the case.

---

[*] *First published in Singapore's Today on 9 April 2009.*

Had this proven true, then some infighting within the PR was to be expected. If the Hindu Rights Action Force, that played such a decisive role in the successes enjoyed by the opposition last year, had been hesitant in its support of Mr Anwar, then one more weak point would have been revealed in the PR.

As things turned out, the Bukit Selambau loss suffered by the BN component party, the Malaysian Indian Congress, is most likely to be the final nail in its coffin.

Nowhere is the running battle between BN and PR more intense than in Perak. Not only is the Bukit Gantang seat a parliamentary one, unlike the other two, the opposition candidate was Mr Mohammad Nazir Jamaluddin, the Chief Minister who was sidelined through BN-orchestrated defections.

The key role played by the Perak sovereign, Sultan Azlan Shah, in naming a new state government to replace the PR, had placed the PR in the difficult position of disobeying him without being disloyal to him. The opposition feared that some rural Malay votes would be lost because of that.

But the result shows that the BN campaign before the by-election to discredit Mr Nazir and branding him a traitor, had indeed failed. This puts further pressure on the Sultan to defuse the crisis in his state by calling for new elections soon.

Had either Bukit Selambau or Bukit Gantang been lost to the BN, there would have been some grounds for Prime Minister Najib Razak's administration to contend that voters were growing disillusioned with the PR.

That would also have given Mr Najib reason to believe that his series of tactical moves was working and would have encouraged him and his advisers to slow the reforming of Umno, the BN and Malaysian governance in general.

The bigger picture after Tuesday's by-elections is that the voter revolt that started in March a year ago has not lessened in strength despite the offensive by the BN.

Alongside aggressive actions such as the power grab in Perak through defections and criminal charges levelled against Mr Anwar and others in the opposition camp, the government's offensive also involved softer tactical moves, such as the release of 13 Internal Security Act detainees; the lifting of a ban on two opposition party newspapers and promises of institutional reforms.

The charm offensive included the return of former Premier Mahathir Mohamed into Umno just in time for him to campaign in Bukit Gantang. But the loss suggests the usefulness of Dr Mahathir may be limited, at least during elections.

The BN can take comfort in that Batang Ai was the first by-election it has won since the general elections. Small comfort perhaps, when one compares with the increased margins with which the PR had won the other four by-elections since that fateful day last year; but it is comfort that comes when it is most needed.

13

Time for Najib to go for broke[*]

SLOGANS don't seem to work. Lifting bans on opposition journals doesn't seem to work. Even releasing detainees held without trial doesn't seem to be working. It seems that whatever approach Malaysia's new Prime Minister Datuk Seri Najib Abdul Razak is being advised to use, is falling flat on its face.

This is because they are meant to be, and are seen as, political spin. With the level of public cynicism towards the political establishment at an all-time high, anything done by the Najib administration that does not immediately cut into the very fabric of the institutions he has promised to reform will be seen as spin.

The Malaysian public has been conscientiously learning how to differentiate spin from sincerity over the last few years, to the extent that any further spin will merely aggravate public cynicism further. The big difference between the first days of Mr Abdullah Badawi and the first days of Mr Najib is that the former came into power on a surge of hope following the retirement of the authoritarian Dr Mahathir Mohamad.

The sense that there was more freedom in the air was strong in 2004. Many wished to believe that Abdullah would – and could – reform the United Malays National Organisation (Umno). People were generous then.

At that time, it was not obvious to the general public how badly the institutions of state, including the dominant Umno, had deteriorated over the last two decades. Instead of the general atmosphere of rejoicing

---

[*] *First published in Singapore's Today on 25 April 2009.*

that followed the end of Mahathirism, we have today cynicism over Umno's ability to correct itself. This cloud of cynicism is so thick, one can cut it with a sheathed keris.

The slogan being parroted by members of Mr Najib's administration – One Malaysia, People First, Performance Now – has been causing a fair share of confusion, accompanied by a great measure of disparagement.

Mr Najib's lifting of the ban on two opposition journals is seen by many as an orchestrated event, as they had been banned a week earlier. Critics argue that this had been done so that the new government could be seen to take it away immediately afterwards.

The release of ISA detainees, though welcomed, is also seen as a superficial gesture that the government is willing to review one of the most controversial and contentious issues in the country.

As was the case with Mr Abdullah, the fear that reforms carried out too fervently will capsize the boat shared by so many power-holders must still exist in the new administration.

Caution is therefore preferred over zeal. Over time, such caution amounts merely to conservatism. If the idea is to convince the public that the new government means business, then it should just carry out serious changes to its institutions and key personnel, instead of talking about doing it.

If he is serious about saving the BN and Umno, Mr Najib should just do it, surprising Umno, the BN, the public and the opposition in the process, leaving them to react as well as they can to it. He has to show daring. The fact that most Malaysians do not believe he has that in him provides a stronger reason for him to rise to the occasion.

Nothing worth doing can be without a backlash, and nothing worth doing can protect all interests. That is the point of reforms. Mr Abdullah was too careful about how reforms would undermine what he saw as the mainstay of his power. Tentativeness led him nowhere.

That is the lesson Mr Najib has to learn from Mr Abdullah's experience. He cannot be authoritarian like Dr Mahathir — that time is gone. He cannot be like Mr Abdullah because we have already had an Abdullah and Malaysians do not seem willing to be as generous towards the BN as they were in 2004.

What Mr Najib is left with, and that is indeed his fate, is that he has very little choice. He has to do to the establishment what the opposition threatens to do, and do it before the opposition has a chance to do it. He has to reform the system no matter what. He has to jump in at the deep end, go for broke, and reform Umno without hesitation.

The trend is towards greater openness in Malaysia. This is not the function of express government policy, necessarily, but because the Malaysian public is feeling a stronger sense of empowerment than it has ever felt before.

What we may expect to see in the near future are mixed signals from the government. The government cannot act like a single integrated unit unless Mr Najib acts the strongman, not against society or the opposition, but against the system that he leads and that put him where he is.

That is what a reformist does. He cleans house, physically and conceptually, starting with his own.

14

The May 13 Legacy*

IT WILL soon be the 40th anniversary of the riots that broke out in Kuala Lumpur at dusk on May 13, 1969.

Not many events have left as strong an imprint on the history and the psyche of the nation as the violence of that evening and the days that followed did.

What exactly happened is still the subject of heated debate among all parties, but often behind closed doors. One could argue that some closure was achieved through the March 8 elections of last year, when the power structure was badly shaken up, just as it was by the May 10 elections of 1969.

The significance of the fact that no inter-racial fighting followed last year's elections should not be underrated. Things have changed. Malaysians accept the results of polls, despite the fact that most of them think the country's free elections may not be exactly fair.

The dramatic change in inter-racial tensions was very noticeable in 1998 at the height of the Reformasi Movement sparked off by the sacking, arrest and trial of former Deputy Prime Minister Anwar Ibrahim.

Suddenly, race did not seem relevant. That movement acted as the universal solvent for many of the suspicions that the various ethnic groups, living under a race-based system of government for half a century, harboured against each other.

____

* *First published in Singapore's Today on 9 May 2009.*

This was most obvious among the young. The important thing that happened between 1998 and 2008 was that the post-May 13 generation managed to convince their elders that new times were at hand.

Looking back today, chances of a new May 13 happening are small. Indeed, they are definitely smaller than rioting aimed at the central government's use of harsh laws to silence dissent.

But the beginnings of closure to May 13 among the people have not been matched by the dismantling of the institutions that stemmed from that dark day.

This is made painfully apparent by the use of the Sedition Act just before May 13, 2009, to justify the arrest of respected activist Wong Chin Huat, a lecturer in journalism at Monash University, Subang.

Mr Wong, who was born in Perak, had acted as spokesperson for Bersih (the Coalition for Free and Clean Elections), in announcing a peaceful protest, through the wearing of black, against the Perak state assembly on Thursday. That assembly would, in effect, finalise the switch in power managed by the federal government against the opposition coalition that won the Perak state election last year.

Significantly, another high-profile case of sedition is to be heard on May 12, involving popular blogger Raja Petra Kamarudin.

What these events highlight, along with the new federal government's weak hints that it will soon review the highly-criticised Internal Security Act (ISA), is that the legacy of May 13 is most poignantly found in the survival of harsh laws put in place after the riots.

Such laws are plentiful, and one does not even have to include the 1971 Constitutional (Amendment) Bill in the discussion.

For one thing, the Emergency (Public Order and Prevention of Crime) Ordinance (EO) passed after May 13, 1969, is still in effect. According to a recent report, this law was responsible for as many as 1,000 or more detainees being held without trial in 2004.

Tough times called for tough laws. In 1971, the Sedition Act that came into being in 1948 to fight Red insurgents was hardened to overrule parliamentary immunity, among other things. This followed the tradition set in 1960 when the ISA was passed to replace the

Emergency Regulations Ordinance of 1948, also originally put in place to fight communist guerrillas.

Apparently, while detention under the ISA is ordered by the Home Ministry and top officials, the EO is purportedly used when insufficient evidence is available to low-level investigators.

Another law is the Printing Ordinance, which was passed in 1948 and was revised in 1971. Dr Mahathir Mohamed transformed it further in 1984 into the Printing Presses and Publications Act, which required the print media to obtain a licence annually.

Another law passed in 1971 was The Universities and University Colleges Act. This piece of legislation serves to drastically limit student involvement in politics.

In 1972, the Official Secrets Act was passed to prohibit the dissemination of any information classified as an official secret. This Act covers a wide range of items, and despite an amendment in 1986, is criticised for muffling the press, stifling dissent and seriously reducing transparency in governance.

Are they still necessary? While a case can certainly be made that these laws did serve a vital function when they were passed, there is a lack of a culture or mechanism to repeal or review such laws.

There are at least two related reasons why the country needs to get over a major trauma like May 13. First, without closure, the inter-ethnic fissures of 1969 will continue to be exploited by parties that otherwise risk irrelevance. Second, without closure, the populace remains limited by — and addicted to — the narrow mindset of those days.

In short, without honest and open discussion about its harshest laws, the country remains in a permanent state of crisis and cannot possibly realise its full potential. Fear remains a constant element in Malaysian politics.

15

The Chin Peng Challenge[*]

THE final attempt by the 85-year-old former leader of the Malayan Communist Party (MCP), Chin Peng, to gain the right to return to Malaysia was quashed on April 30 by the Federal Court.

His failure to produce his birth certificate was used as sufficient reason to deny his appeal.

The legal technicalities involved in stopping him from entering the country are interestingly not the most significant theme in this saga. His failure nevertheless injects disturbing elements from the past into contemporary Malaysian consciousness.

Many see no danger in allowing the old man to return from his place of exile in Bangkok to his place of birth in Sitiawan, Perak, where many of his relatives live, but others, including the federal authorities, refuse to forget the violence perpetrated by the MCP during the birth of the nation.

The official stand is taken despite the peace agreement signed between the MCP and government on Dec 2, 1989, stating that party members who were of Malaysian origin should be allowed to settle in the country if they wished to do so.

Chin Peng's mistake was that he did not take up then Premier Mahathir Mohamed on that offer immediately.

This article was written in remembrance of the late Andrew Symon, with whom the writer had many discussions about Chin Peng. First published in Singapore's Today on 23 May 2009.

Much of the reluctance to allow him to return stems from challenges that are embodied in Chin Peng's very existence, to official discourses about the origins of Malaysian independence.

Firstly, communists such as Chin Peng (real name Ong Boon Hua) were practically the only Malayans fighting the Japanese invaders during World War II. They did it with material and logistical support from British defenders who had recently so hastily abandoned their colonies in South-east Asia.

Chin Peng is therefore a reminder of a fractious time when the Japanese were seen as invaders by some but as liberators of Malaya from British control by others.

The portrayal of communists as terrorists was therefore a narrative device that served to depict British colonialists as defenders of decent government, protectors of the public and willing participants in bringing independence to Malaya, in the final days of their empire.

Willing participants in this project where the local population was concerned — once the communists had been dismissed by British commissioner-general in South-east Asia Malcolm McDonald as "alien forces acting under alien instructions" — were solely conservative parties such as the United Malays National Organisation (Umno) and the Malayan Chinese Association (MCA).

Indeed, the forming of the MCA in 1949 was a measure deemed necessary by the British and by Chinese Malayan leaders to draw rural support away from the communists after the former decided on guerilla warfare against their erstwhile brothers-in-arms.

Chin Peng's continued intrusion into Malaysian consciousness also conjure discomforting images of a time when the fire of nationalism throughout the colonised world was inextricably alloyed with the promise of liberation from the colonial yoke and the building of a paradise based on economic equality and social justice without regard for national borders.

An alien force

Had the communists of pre-independence Malaya not be perceived as aliens with an agenda countervailing against the nationalism of the conservative parties of the alliance — to whom independence was finally given by the British — then the whole understanding of Malaysian history would have to be revised.

That will not doubt make Malaysia's history more interesting, but that would also challenge the narrower narratives that we have grown contented with.

Admitting the full mix of passions in the twilight years of British might, and the blend of aspirations found among peoples filled with the vision that they could finally escape colonial control, would allow us today to entertain ideas that are not so strongly nationalistic, ethnocentric or parochial.

A proper study of the post-war period would also reveal a high level of economic duress among urban and rural Malayans. This would go some way towards explaining the officially-assumed political disinterest among most non-Malay Malayans of that time in the process of Merdeka.

The race-based nature of Malaysia's official history is largely a result of the depiction of the MCP as an alien force that carried little significance in the ideological dynamics of Merdeka.

Through a concentration on the racial nature of major parties, which also avoided the fact that non-conservative parties were not included in negotiations with the British, the conceptual space for race politics was advertently enlarged.

Precisely through the branding of class struggle on the national stage as a sideshow, Merdeka basically became an ethnocentric struggle that has informed Malaysian political thought every since.

Permitting Chin Peng to return would amount to an admission by officialdom that he and his buddies were part of the struggles of the immediate post-war period, and that the left-right political dimension that consumed world politics during that age — which was a major motivation for the British to orchestrate their withdrawal from the region the way they did — was also very much a part of Malaysian political thought.

16

Is the future for PAS to lose?*

WITH the new distribution of voter sympathies in Malaysia that became evident in the general elections last year, the country's major parties found themselves in a state of uncertainty.

This was, and is, true both of the winners and the losers. However, in the foreseeable future, how the losers transform themselves will not be as interesting as how the winners adapt themselves to their new-found prominence. This prominence has continued to grow, if one is to judge from the dominance that the opposition parties have shown in all by-elections – except one – since then.

Immediately after the March 8 elections last year, most of the attention was on the ruling United Malays National Organisation (Umno). The party was like a giant hit between the eyes. Although it reeled, it did not fall. Fifteen months down the road, we see that the chances of that party transforming itself into something very different from what it had been over the last few decades are small.

The new premier, Najib Abdul Razak, has over the last two months not shown the depth of understanding of the situation that is required for him to take the necessary risks involved in transforming the party and the ruling coalition into a creature that can better represent the new socio-economic and socio-political entity that Malaysia has evolved into over the last twenty years.

---

* *First published in Singapore's Today and in The Malaysian Insider on 6 June 2009.*

Umno's allies on the peninsula, in a delayed reaction to their losses, are all presently going through internal turmoil. The PPP is split, the MIC is split, the Gerakan is split and the MCA is split.

Umno's split involved the silencing of moderate tendencies with the sacking of Zaid Ibrahim, the former law minister, from the party.

Interestingly, it is also becoming clear to members of the alternative coalition, the Pakatan Rakyat, that they need to be responsive to the new demands their new prominence places on them.

The greatest challenge seems to be that of personnel. No doubt, the BN lost much ground in the general elections due to the fact that its personnel were of increasingly low quality. Since they benefited greatly from this BN's weakness, Pakatan parties now live with the pressure of showing that their people were essentially better than BN's people.

The Perak state assemblymen from PKR and DAP jumping ship to join the Barisan Nasional and toppling the Pakatan government there in the process have been the most dramatic cases opposition failure to maintain quality and loyalty in the ranks.

But it is not only about having good people. It is about having federally electable people, and especially about having a federally acceptable agenda. On that score, Parti Islam SeMalaysia (PAS) faces the biggest challenge.

And often mentioned point about politics in Malaysia is that all the race-based parties were founded before independence was achieved in 1957. All these parties are members of the BN, except for PAS, which, though a religious party, is functionally a race party.

The allies it has, and which it needs if it is to increase in significance in the immediate future, are multiracial parties formed after independence.

And so, its transformation is a difficult one. Can it shed its reputation as a race-biased party and turn into one that – though religious – is race-blind?

This is the great significance of the party elections now taking place. On it hangs not only the future of PAS, but of Pakatan as a whole.

Where BN is concerned, a clear victory for the ulama leadership will be welcome news.

17

The transformation of PAS has just begun*

THE national attention given the general assembly of the Islamist PAS held recently was a historical high for the party.

This certainly confirms the fact that PAS is enjoying a level of popularity that it has not experienced in its 58 years of existence. However, much of this popularity is incidental, and more serious internal change is needed if the party is to take full advantage of its new status.

Umno, from which more religiously inclined Malays broke away in 1951 to form PAS, is losing credibility fast. Furthermore, it has not been able to reverse the trend despite changes in its top leadership.

Since Malaysia has a Muslim-Malay majority, PAS is therefore well placed to benefit from this, and will continue to attract Muslim and Malay votes in the near future. In fact, support for PAS has been growing at a phenomenal rate ever since former premier Tun Dr Mahathir Mohamad went overboard in quashing the career of his erstwhile deputy Datuk Seri Anwar Ibrahim in 1998, and now boasts almost one million members.

The rift in the Malay community created by Mahathir's harsh methods did not only undermine the Islamic credentials of Umno, especially in rural areas, they also alienated the party from the urban young of all races and genders.

* *First published in The Malaysian Insider on 10 June 2009.*

Except for the period of promise offered by Tun Abdullah Ahmad Badawi in 2004, young Malay men and women in the cities have been showing a preference for Anwar's Parti Keadilan Rakyat (PKR). PAS, at the same time, has been gaining strength in rural areas. These two parties provide the major alternatives for Malays disaffected with Umno.

By going into a coalition with the nominally social-democratic DAP, these two parties now command enough support to give the ruling Barisan Nasional coalition a run for its money.

The enormous support that PAS received from Chinese voters in the recent Bukit Gantang by-election was thus more an expression of the hope that Pakatan Rakyat is a viable alternative than the supposed direct acceptance of PAS by non-Muslims which encouraged PAS to wish to upgrade its non-Muslim supporter club into an official wing of the party.

But PAS is still basically a rural-based party that challenges Umno on its home turf. Should the young PKR develop well as a responsible party over the coming months, it will come to stand as the major alternative for young urban Malays looking for a political domicile outside of Umno.

With the urban population of the country growing in strength and the average age of voters dropping sharply, PKR does actually have an edge over PAS in the long term. Whether or not, the division within PAS should be termed "clerics" versus "professionals", or "ulamas" versus "Erdogans", Malaysian society itself, and therefore the voter population as well, is dividing itself along the dimensions of age, the level of education and the level of urbanity.

These undermine the potency of race-speak and religion-speak.

PAS's surprise call for the Sisters in Islam (SIS) to be banned illustrates the fact that change will not come easily to the party, and that the dissonance between the party's old roots and society's new shoots is very real.

Indeed, the very existence of Pakatan and the recent success of its component parties were possible because of the aforementioned social dynamics. The Reformasi movement that started in 1998 inspired many young Malaysians into realising how out-of-touch with their aspirations old parties like Umno and its allies had become. There is therefore a lot of hope-against-hope amongst voters where PAS — one of the oldest parties in Malaysia — is concerned.

It is being given the benefit of the doubt, at least for the time being.

New social changes in Malaysia demand new political expressions and the parties that attune themselves quickly to them are the ones to gain most from it. That is how democracy works at its most basic level.

The older a party is, the stronger the obsession with past self-identities and the harder it finds it to adapt to new social dynamics. The advantage PAS has nationally over Umno is that it is untainted by power, but like Umno, it is hampered by the false impression that change can be on its own terms.

After the trashing it received at the hands of Abdullah in 2004, PAS did reinvent itself to an extent. It was therefore sufficiently well positioned to profit from the broad rejection of the Umno-led coalition when that came in 2008.

Given the great expectations voters now have on the Pakatan Rakyat, the most difficult part of the act of transformation lies ahead, especially for an old party like PAS.

18

Making incumbency count[*]

AFTER being in top-level politics for 34 years, Malaysia's new Prime Minister, Najib Abdul Razak, the eldest son of the popular second Prime Minister, Abdul Razak Hussein, must have imagined better conditions for his long-awaited rise to the political summit.

Najib took over on 3 April – just about 100 days ago – after the United Malays National Organization (Umno) finally decided that it could not afford to accommodate former premier Abdullah Badawi's wish to stay on for half his term following the trouncing suffered by the party and its allies in the general elections of March 8, 2008.

Needless to say, there was considerable bad blood involved in Abdullah's departure. This was most evident in Najib's exclusion of Abdullah's son-in-law, Khairy Jamaluddin, from his Cabinet, despite the young man being elected as chief of the influential Umno Youth. To add salt to injury, Khairy's deputy, Razali Ibrahim, was made a deputy minister, as was one of the two candidates that Khairy had defeated – Mukhriz Mahathir.

Major attempts have been made to give Sabah Umno an over-representation in the corridors of power. Most would agree that East Malaysia's two states hold the key to power in the foreseeable future, and are able to tilt the balance as they please.

What Najib also noted was that his party and his allies were not capable of winning any important by-election for the time being. Over the last three months, five by-elections have been held. Four of these

---

[*]   *First published in OpinionAsia.com on 10 July 2009.*

were on the peninsula, and the three in which Umno and its allies contested, were won with increased margins by the opposition, the Pakatan Rakyat (PR). Things looked so hopeless that Umno decided, for the first time ever, not to field a candidate in the fourth case.

Public sympathy, especially among the young, remains strongly with the opposition. Najib's messy success in toppling the PR government in the state of Perak through crossovers has not endeared him to voters.

The lesson he quickly had to learn was that a blow-for-blow war against the opposition would only leave Umno and its allies with an increasingly bloody nose.

The areas in which he could instead make incumbency count and steer from a position of strength are in foreign relations and in the management of the country's macro-economics.

Najib's significant overseas trips were to Singapore and China. The first trip involved attracting Singaporean investments to Malaysia but ended up being remembered for the controversy it generated about the building of a third bridge between the two countries, which he had ill-advisedly proposed.

His trip to China was engineered to be seen on all sides as a journey in the footsteps of his illustrious father, who went to China as part of a process of mutual diplomatic recognition between the two countries, and to gain support from Beijing for Malaysia's neutrality policy for Southeast Asia.

Najib has been able to gain significant publicity points from his visit to China, especially among Chinese Malaysians, who are almost certainly his major subject for courtship at the moment. He has promised news of major Chinese investments in the country in the new future.

Where economic policies in general are concerned, the two stimulus packages he had stringed together as Finance Minister since November 2008 of RM67 billion have been lacking in details, and have not been generating the public confidence he had hoped for. In the meantime, the forecast for the country's GDP contraction has been getting more negative, and is presently at 5%.

Just in time to provide positive material for analysts and pundits waiting to announce their judgment on his first 100 days as premier, however, Najib announced some radical measures that are undoubtedly generating a huge amount of national and international interest.

Exactly 88 days after coming to power, he reduced significantly rules and conditions surrounding bumiputera ownership and participation, and property transactions involving bumiputeras. This move came two months after his decision to lift the 30-percent bumiputera equity rule in 27 service sectors. That had removed restrictions on foreign investment in health and social services, tourism, transport, computer and other related sectors. Another initiative raised the cap on foreign ownership of investment banks and insurers to 70%, and also relaxed rules governing the granting of banking licenses.

Despite strong suspicions among many, including his temperamental mentor, Mahathir Mohamed, that his latest initiatives at de-radicalizing investment terms were timed more for boosting his flagging popularity than as essential steps in a comprehensive reform of the national economic infrastructure, there were momentous enough to excite even local skeptics.

In contrast, his inaugural speech made 100 days ago which announced the release of 13 detainees held under the Internal Security Act, the lifting of a ban on two opposition publications and the review of the ISA itself, did not work well. That event was perceived to have been too blatantly choreographed to manipulate public sentiments in his favour.

The key question now is: Are we seeing the beginning of the end for the controversial affirmative action programme, the New Economic Policy? Answering that question, and handling other hot potatoes like the ISA, the Umno electoral system and police reforms will keep him occupied for the next 100 days.

19

Populism has its redeeming points*

MALAYSIAN Prime Minister Mohd Najib Abdul Razak will have been in power 100 days tomorrow.

Strongly conscious of the appraisals that will come unbidden from all directions to mark the day, he announced his decision to liberalise the economy just over a week ago. Undoubtedly, this forces his critics to exercise more nuance than they are used to doing.

There are precedents to such tactical orchestrations. In fact, when Najib took over office on April 3 from the hapless Abdullah Badawi, he used the occasion to declare the release of 13 detainees held without trial under the Internal Security Act (ISA), the ban on two opposition publications, and a review of the controversial ISA itself.

The ban on the publications had been placed only a week earlier.

Though largely welcomed, his latest moves to invigorate the economy, which include the removal of directives governing equity acquisition, mergers and takeovers as well the lowering of quotas to favour Malays, caused expected discomfort in the ranks of his party, the United Malays National Organisation (Umno).

Most notably, former Prime Minister Mahathir Mohamad, now strangely one of Malaysia's top bloggers, suggested that Najib's new initiative was aimed at winning popularity for the new administration more than for its macro-economic efficacy.

---

* *First published in Singapore's Today on 11 July 2009.*

Though relatively softly worded, Mahathir's criticism continues a stream of negative reactions he has had to earlier moves by Najib. The prime minister's idea for a third bridge to Singapore has not been acceptable to Mahathir, nor the encouragement he has given for so-called "unity talks" with Parti Islam SeMalaysia.

Najib's problems are as profound as his to-do list is long. His tasks facing him include seriously reforming Umno and the Barisan Nasional, keeping the opposition at bay, attracting young voters, regaining the support of non-Malays for his coalition, and reducing the local effects of the global crisis.

And he has to do all this without upsetting the already apprehensive Malay constituency too much.

Keeping many balls in the air is never easy, especially when you have to keep adding more balls in the meantime. In lieu of an all-encompassing ideology or a comprehensive master plan, this career politician cannot but offer reforms in an apparent ad hoc manner.

Given such a scenario, it is indeed gratifying to see that his administration is thinking up measures designed to make him popular. The alternatives are not desirable. The use of sharp elbows, as in the takeover of power in Perak state, damaged Najib's reputation severely. Intimidation through the use of Draconian laws and police force, the means preferred last year by Syed Hamid Albar, Abdullah's last home affairs minister, merely came across as vile desperation on the part of a status quo.

In the long run, a reformist is as a reformist does. By pinching points from the opposition's agenda, as he is now doing, Najib will inevitably bring confusion to its ranks, not that those ranks need any help in being confused at the moment.

Populism has its uses, as even Mahathir himself would know. As long as Najib feels that reforms will gain him mileage with voters, his administration is less prone to adopt ruthless methods against social forces seeking change.

No doubt, such a tactic dilutes the effect of each reform attempted. The main objection to Najib's reforms – which as yet do not include reforming the police, the electoral system or the judiciary, and reviewing harsh laws – is that their implementation cannot succeed because they start at the wrong end.

Mahathir's point should be well taken by the prime minister. The lack of a holistic approach to reforms belies the lack of a broad understanding of the problems the country faces. These include systematic corruption within the civil service, in business practices, in resource redistribution, in the awarding of projects, in law enforcement and within the major ruling parties themselves.

Najib's wish to democratize the electoral system of Umno, which may actually lessen vote-buying in this powerful party, therefore bears watching.

A blow-by-blow exchange with his opponents on the arena of domestic politics has for three years been a bad tactic for Umno to use. It would be wise in that light for him to have the charge of sodomy against opposition leader Anwar Ibrahim dropped. He has no political points to gain there any longer.

A much better chance of attaining popularity – given the resistance to change among his own people – is through tactically chosen piecemeal reforms. The focus of these reforms is in the area of foreign affairs and macro-economics, and the benefits he expects from them at the local level have to flow indirectly from this.

From his present position of strength, he can steer and command in ways that are beyond his opponents to do.

His visits to China and to Singapore and his overtures to the leaders of these countries, along with the recent relaxing of investment regulations, issue from this rationale. His target is the non-Malay voter. Given the popularity contest that Mahathir so rightly identifies him to be in, one may expect Najib to take off his reformist hat any day soon, when Malay resistance has grown too loud.

20

"Remember Beng Hock" will be a steady battle cry[*]

WHATEVER support Datuk Seri Najib Razak managed to gain for himself with his recent attempts at reforms has now gone out the window along with Teoh Beng Hock.

Teoh, the political secretary to Selangor DAP exco member Ean Yong Hian Wah, was found dead on a neighbouring rooftop below the Malaysian Anti-Corruption Commission's building in Shah Alam on July 16. According to reports, he had endured 10 hours of questioning by the MACC throughout the previous night.

Later that afternoon, his body was discovered on the roof of the adjacent building. The police have quickly announced that there is no evidence of foul play

Teoh was apparently not even a suspect in the MACC's fervent operation recently launched against Selangor state assemblymen belonging to the Pakatan Rakyat (PR) coalition. What makes his death more painfully tragic is that Teoh's fiancée is pregnant, and the couple was scheduled to register his marriage the following day.

Given the lack of public confidence in the police, the anti-corruption apparatus and the federal government itself, calls for a thorough investigation by an independent commission into the case can be expected for a long time to come.

____

* *First published in The Malaysian Insider on 20 July 2009.*

When the anger and sadness that this incident is generating subsides, the fingers of blame cannot but point beyond the MACC officers involved, and at Najib himself. He will be called upon to clarify why his party and coalition should not bear the responsibility for failing to reform the police and the anti-corruption authorities from the bottom up, as recommended by an endless number of experts.

The suspicion will grow that the federal government under Najib — judging from the mix of tactical reforms and sly politicking — does not appreciate how badly compromised the federal apparatus actually is. Despite continuous defeats at the polls, his administration has continued to treat the success of the opposition as if it were the result of clever tactics on the part of Datuk Seri Anwar Ibrahim and his allies, and not as a public outcry for clean and reliable government.

Criticism that his recent reforms are cosmetic and more tactical than sincere will continue to grow. Given the difficult times that the Pakatan Rakyat has had in recent weeks, Teoh's death provides renewed focus for its disheartened supporters.

Unlike the few recent cases of deaths under police custody, this one at the Selangor MACC headquarters involves a young man known for his political engagement. His demise therefore carries great political implications, and will be a milestone in the nation's painful history that future students of Malaysia will have to commit to memory for their exams.

It is a tipping point. "Remember Teo Beng Hock" will be a battle cry for a long time to come.

The ball has now landed squarely in Najib's court. If he is serious about reforming Malaysia beyond foreign investment regulations and quota changes, he now has his chance of putting partisanship aside, seizing the moment, and acting as a national leader who realises how vital the integrity and professionalism of its investigative authorities are.

Teoh's death is too big to be swept under the carpet, and will continue to arouse anger unless properly investigated. And even then, strong demands for some decisive action on the government's part to make sure that no such thing will happen again are to be expected.

Needless to say, the many young activists who have arisen since the Reformasi movement started in 1998 will sympathise at a personal level with Teoh's family. As long as the case is not openly cleared up, the misgiving will remain strong that it could have been any one of them who might have suffered — or may suffer — an end similar to Teoh's.

Just a day before Teoh died, the ruling Barisan Nasional was asserting that the narrow margin of 65 votes with which it lost to PR in the Manek Urai by-election showed that the pendulum that had been swinging in PR's favour for two years was now going the other way.

Indeed, Najib's popularity had risen sharply according to a recent survey done by the Merdeka Center. Teoh's death sends a reminder to voters that the police and the anti-corruption body are in pressing need of serious reforming. For PR supporters, their resolve to work for a change of federal government will be strengthened.

What one must conclude from this incident is that Najib's chosen course of reform avoids his major challenge, which is to restore the credibility of the police, the judiciary and the anti-corruption apparatus.

As long as he sidesteps this duty, his other attempts at change will not be taken seriously. Indeed, even his allies within BN are feeling a greater need to put pressure publicly on Najib.

For starters, it would be wise of Najib to call off MACC's blatant campaign against the Selangor government.

21

Teoh's case stems from disregard of due process*

THE Rule of Law cannot exist without the understanding that Justice is Blind.

But why must Justice be blind to exist, we may ask? Clearly, that is because its objectivity would be immediately compromised.

Justice, however, is not merely a court matter. For blindness to be ubiquitous in the courts of a country, respect for the rule of law must be fostered throughout the executive and the legislative arms of government as well as the judiciary. Knowing that humans are prone to biases, philosophers of law have arrived at the conclusion that incorporating checks and balances into the system is the surest way of neutralizing this human weakness.

The rule of law is more than just a technical matter, however. It is a cultural phenomenon that takes time to inculcate, and that requires steady political will to achieve.

That is why the sudden death of Teoh Beng Hock, the political aide to an executive council member in Selangor state, carries such heavy political implications for Malaysia.

A witness – not an accused – taken in for questioning by his country's anti-graft body should not have to fear that his fundamental rights will be trodden upon. He certainly should not fear losing his life.

---

* *First published in Singapore's Today on 25 July 2009.*

But while apparently still under the protection of the Malaysian Anti-Corruption Commission (MACC), to whose headquarters he was taken on the late afternoon of 16 July, Teoh died.

The 30-year-old was found on the fifth floor of a building adjacent to the MACC offices in Shah Alam at 1.30pm the following day. An initial autopsy report says that he had been dead for about 5 hours when his body was discovered.

Evidence found around him suggests that he had fallen from the 14th floor, which is occupied by the MACC, and not from the unused 9th floor, as had been reported earlier. He had been interrogated throughout the night for at least nine hours, and probably for much longer.

Outraged further by the fact that Teoh was scheduled to register his marriage on the day he died, and that his fiancée was two months into her pregnancy, many Malaysians have been finding it hard to contain their anger over the past week.

Teoh's case acts not only as a painful reminder of recent cases of people dying while under police custody, but also of the fact that the government had been ignoring those cases. A pattern of incompetence and arrogance born of sustained non-accountability among public servants now appears too clear for Malaysians to ignore.

Arbitrariness in the implementation of the law is a fearsome thing. It is not for no reason a reliable tool of torturers. It is such a horrendous thing that the government that does not curb the human desire to abuse the law among its many servants loses its legitimacy in the eyes of the public.

The Teoh case, happening so unexpectedly and right in the middle of an anti-corruption campaign against the Selangor state government, leaves the federal government and its many arms without moral defence, and with no choice but to accede to popular demands.

These demands are basically that a royal commission be formed to investigate Teoh's death. Any hint of a cover-up in this case is bound to backfire on the police and the government very quickly. Unsurprisingly, most parties involved are already expressing support for such a commission.

The Cabinet finally acted seven days after Teoh's death. It acceded to public demand but in a reluctant fashion. Some of the MACC officers involved in the case are being transferred, and not suspended; while a royal commission is to be formed to look into MACC investigative procedures and to determine if any human right violations were committed during Teoh's interrogation, and not specifically to investigate Teoh's death.

But even a royal commission will not dissipate the distrust of the continuously outraged. The government's handling of royal commission reports in recent years has not been encouraging. Their recommendations tend to be ignored, or at least watered down considerably.

The major problem remains. Suspicions of the authorities run deep. That distrust is indeed as much a part of Malaysian culture as the insulation from accountability among public officials is a part of the country's bureaucratic culture. One mirrors the other.

Only a sincere leader can break that vicious circle. Respect for the rule of law at various levels takes a long time to re-instill in society. It has to be fostered by consistent action from the top, both in meting out punishment and in setting an example for others to follow.

A steady erosion of respect for the rule of law has been going on in Malaysia at least since the 1980s. We are seeing its undeniable effects now. Indeed, one cannot expect respect for the rule of law in the judiciary, for example, if a culture of decency, legality and accountability is not prevalent in the executive and the legislative arms of government as well.

The sorry predicament that Malaysians have to face today is: How is one to abide by the law when the law seems arbitrarily applied by its purported guardians?

22

Let's all be 1Malaysians already*

THE term "1Malaysia" being promulgated by Prime Minister Najib Abdul Razak's administration has been generating steady ridicule and heated debate ever since he became Malaysia's leader over three months ago.

Much of the controversy stems from the fact that he will not admit that "1Malaysia" must come close to the notion of "Malaysian Malaysia" in meaning if not in words. But let us sidestep prickly trouble by avoiding the latter phrase coined over 40 years ago, and concentrate on "1Malaysia" instead.

We can all agree that what is being demanded of individual Malaysians today, either by the aging Barisan Nasional or by the infant Pakatan Rakyat, is for Malaysians to reflect more deeply on their role in creating a peaceful and prosperous country, and then to exercise active acceptance of ethnic or religious differences.

However, in order to kick-start that process, the government has to show in indubitable ways that Malaysians are equal before the law. That is a necessary step to take. As long as the belief is strong in Malaysians that Malaysian law in practice is not reliable, the government is not fair and justice is not blind, then 1Malaysia remains an empty slogan.

However, the long-term project of achieving inter-communal harmony should not be ridiculed. In the absence of a definite vision among its leaders, what Malaysians need to do as individuals is to start acting like citizens of whatever future Malaysia they wish to be a part

---

* *First published in The Malaysian Insider on 30 July 2009.*

of. Let us all be 1Malaysians already – or Malaysian Malaysians if you prefer – and not wait too long for a harmonious society to descend from above.

As the prime minister himself has claimed, the Government Knows Best era is over, which means it is time for citizens to get into the act and participate actively in creating a harmonious, confident and progressive society.

But what can this 1Malaysian be? And what harmony are we envisaging?

Even if we cannot be expected to agree on how we are to be such a thing, we can at least adopt the attitudes that are becoming of sincere proponents of a harmonious Malaysia.

A lot of inspiration can in fact be drawn from past attempts at national harmony, such as the Rukunegara born of the sufferings of May 13; Mahathir Mohamed's Way Forward envisaging a globalized Malaysian economy and citizenry; and even Abdullah Badawi's badly maligned Islam Hadhari.

The Rukunegara – publicized on National Day 1971 – simply states that the country is dedicated to the achieving of certain goals. These can be turned bottoms up, and just as profitably be reviewed as individual goals, and not merely state-directed abstractions.

Sharply paraphrased, an individual following the Rukunegara does not put imagined group rights and interests before him/herself. Such a person (1) exhibits a liberal acceptance of diverse cultures and religions; (2) struggles for a just, egalitarian and democratic society; and (3) seeks greater understanding of modern science and technology. National unity is then the indirect end result of sufficient citizens adopting such liberal and progressive attitudes.

Mahathir's Vision 2020 – announced in 1991 – is definitely wordier than the Rukunegara, and employs terms that are useful because they are vague. Nevertheless, one can extract certain central tenets from it that can be inspirational for the individual 1Malaysian.

The 1Malaysian – or the member of Bangsa Malaysia, if one prefers – pursues excellence with full confidence and with pride in himself and his country, behaves democratically, holds himself to high ethical standards, feels that he/she belongs to the nation despite his/her cultural exceptionality, contributes to the scientific and technological civilization that awaits mankind, is family-oriented, cares for the welfare of others and seeks to reduce economic inequality, and works hard.

We could continue along the series of national ideologies and even adopt ideas from Abdullah Badawi's Islam Hadhari for the 1Malaysian to use, irrespectively of his or her religion. From the Abdullah period, he/she can adopt the ideal of fighting for the rights of minority groups and of safeguarding the environment.

Since the 1Malaysian strives for the betterment of society, the environment and him/herself, and does this among fellow 1Malaysians who are markedly different in all sorts of ways, the harmony of the 1Malaysia of the future must build more on Rejoicing in Diversity than on Unity in Diversity.

Politically, this means that the Federation of Malaysia, to be more at peace with itself, must be less centrally controlled for all 1Malaysians to feel at peace with themselves and their nation. Less Centralism, More Unity.

23

Reformist conservatives versus conservative reformists[*]

ALL parties agree on one thing in Malaysia at the moment, and that is that things are in flux.

The politically positive trend is to talk about "reforms". This is due to the huge demonstrations the country has witnessed lately, and the impressive victories won by opposition parties in recent elections. Nevertheless, the political bedrock is very much a conservative one, in some areas extremely so.

Indeed, in the lull between general elections, conservatives tend to have an easy time, wanting as they always do for inevitable change to come minimally and slowly.

Keeping the pace slow while making it seem fast, is the best possible tactic.

Those seeking change have a harder time since they wish for something that is not already in existence and that therefore is harder for the popular mind to imagine. How much more troublesome it is to promulgate change to a crowd grown proud of being cynical.

When external forces signal turbulent times and internal forces cry for reforms, there are two things conservatives can do. They can crush the reformists by violent means — which can always be kept as the last option — or they can announce strategically chosen reforms to

<hr>

* *First published in Singapore's Today and in The Malaysian Insider on 19 August 2009.*

appease the many, and then delay and postpone their implementation to hoodwink the rest.

When conservatives initiate reforms, one must assume that they are doing it awfully grudgingly.

Malaysia's Prime Minister Najib Abdul Razak has never been known as a reformist. He is now in control of a powerful apparatus of power that cannot but be conservative after having held power for over 50 years. He thus takes command at a time of reform, just as his predecessor Abdullah Badawi did five years ago.

Najib is therefore wont to choose his reforms carefully. This he has done. He concentrates understandably on foreign affairs and foreign investments. His forays into internal affairs have consistently seen him losing to the opposition in most cases. This downward trend for the ruling coalition was already obvious during Abdullah Badawi's last two years in power.

In contrast to Najib, though, Abdullah's announced areas of reform in his first year in power were in internal affairs. He sought to fight corruption and he sought — apparently very seriously at first — to reform the police. It can be argued that had he carried out a proper restructuring of the police force, he might have increased by 2008 the record popularity he enjoyed in 2004.

But he hesitated, and reversed his decisions. The forces of conservatism within the coalition were too strong. The police did not reform, and corruption grew worst. Abdullah, overseeing this sad trend, thus went from being the most popular leader ever to being the most disappointing.

In that sense, Najib is a more serious conservative than Abdullah. He has cleverly avoided threatening the police, and has instead gone for reforms that do not affect the common man too painfully. Indeed, the writing on the wall says that the unpopular Inspector-General of Police Musa Hassan will stay another term come September.

At least during the first 100 days in power, Najib seemed to have pulled off the difficult trick of appearing a reformist without upsetting conservative supporters too much. His popularity has risen, and the opposition is left somewhat flat-footed.

But then came the unfortunate death of Teoh Beng Hock, a political aide within the opposition party, the DAP. The many rallies that followed were soon accompanied by the huge anti-ISA demonstration on 1 August marking the 49th anniversary of the draconian law. The police, given the green light by Najib and Home Minister Hishammuddin Hussein, used water cannons and tear gas freely.

In forcing the government to show its muscles, the opposition managed to remind erstwhile supporters that nothing had changed, and that the most needed reforms have not been carried out, and are in fact not even on the government's agenda.

Conservatism in these times of change is not found only among those in power. Malaysians are also being given rude reminders that the Islamist party, PAS, despite its recent success in appearing as a dynamic party interpreting Islam as a vehicle for creating good governance in a multiracial country, and not as a mere sanctioning ideology, is having trouble changing its spots.

In its recent party elections, the influence that the ulamas still hold within the party became clear for all to see. The call to ban Sisters in Islam and the attempt to ban alcohol in Selangor state threw strong doubts on the viability of the Pakatan Rakyat (PR) coalition in the longer term.

These reformists are turning out to be as conservative as the conservatives are trying to appear reform-minded.

Harangued by the sodomy charge against Anwar Ibrahim, having lost Perak, and being assailed both in Penang and Selangor, which they control, the PR is being forced to take concrete steps to find common ground beyond mere anti-BN-ness.

Malaysia's nascent two-coalition system is caught in a new balance. On one side, Umno/BN needs to stay conservative without seeming so, while the PR's strategy is to force BN's hand in the areas where reform is most required.

Forcing the police to act, whether on the streets or through arrests and trials, the opposition keeps alive the real conflict between the two sides, which is, the rule of law.

24

Can Najib drop 'Malays' from Umno?*

MALAYSIAN Prime Minister Najib Abdul Razak is reportedly trying to get his Cabinet to drop the requirement for Malaysians to state their race in official documents.

This is a positive move but it raises questions about how far the government is willing to go in tackling Malaysia's principal quandary, and whether it realises how deep the race-related crevices actually are.

Getting rid of the mention of "race" in official documents is the simplest, and most easily-enforced measure the government could take to hint at the direction it wants to go.

The problem is that it is a hint, and measures that merely hint at changes under-rate the enormity of the issue and throw doubt on the establishment's willingness to force Malaysians to rise above race.

It is a drop in the ocean, and the racial ocean is one that is expanding by the day.

The recent rally against the Internal Security Act (ISA) was perplexingly criticised for attacking Malay rights.

Similarly, the anger against the death of opposition political aide Teoh Beng Hock while under interrogation by the Malaysian Anti-Corruption Commission, was also spun incomprehensibly as aggression against a Malay institution.

---

* *First published in Singapore's Today and in The Malaysian Insider on 22 August 2009.*

Race has been a growing issue since the early 1900s, and as the British withdrew, we witnessed the rise of parties with names like the Malayan Indian Congress (MIC), the United Malays National Organisation (Umno) and the Malayan Chinese Association (MCA). The only parties that consciously steered clear of race and religion were left-leaning ones.

Clearly multi-racial parties managed to challenge the Alliance coalitional model of race-based parties in the 1960s. This thrust was however defused after the race riots of May 13, 1969. Several of these parties were quickly incorporated into the coalition, leaving diehards such as the Democratic Action Party championing the multi-racial discourse.

There were good reasons why the affirmative action programme - the New Economic Policy (NEP) - implemented in 1970 had a 20-year limit put on it. The racial problems facing the country were diagnosed to be socio-economic, and not ideological in nature. That was a revolutionary shift in thinking.

However, the remedy for such a complicated and divisive socio-economic ailment, required meticulous application.

Comprehensive government measures to improve the lot of the majority Malay community so that racialism would lose its socio-economic basis ran the risk of popularising racialism as an ideology.

The formulators of the NEP realised that clearly, and therefore prescribed that the medication be stopped after 20 years.

The late Deputy Prime Minister and Home Affairs Minister Ismail Abdul Rahman described the NEP as a golf handicap that one worked towards getting rid of, while Mr Ghazali Shafie, who succeeded him as Home Affairs Minister, is on record as saying that if the NEP had not worked after 20 years, then obviously it would have to be revised or repealed.

Most Malaysians today will have difficulty believing this, but the aim of the NEP was to reduce, not boost, racialism in Malaysian life.

On that score, the NEP has definitely failed.

The medication has led to a serious addiction, and many institutions and individuals are now dependent on the resultant racialism for their power and legitimacy.

Thus, if Mr Najib wants to break his people's dependence on racialism, he needs to be as radical in getting rid of the NEP as his father Abdul Razak Hussein was in putting it into place.

The day he gets his Cabinet to drop "Malays" from Umno, "Chinese" from MCA and "Indian" from MIC will be the day Malaysia finally grows up.

25

The last pickings of race ideology[*]

THANKS to the bloody war against Nazi Germany, Britain evolved in the history books from being a global empire that rationalized its conquests with ideas of racism into being the destroyer of racism.

This is one of the greatest paradoxes of modern history, and there is certainly a lot we can learn from it about the writing of history and about how global paradigms actually do shift, especially when blood has flowed.

After the horrors of racism came home to roost in Europe in the 1930s and 1940s, and tens of millions had died in the process, European mainstream politics could no longer make use of the notion of "race". From 1945 onwards, little support could be gained for arguments about purity of blood, and the notion of race in general.

"Race" quickly became a political taboo in the continent of its birth.

In sync with the fall of racism and the discrediting of racialism, the empires of the West crumbled like black-and-white domino bricks. Throughout the world, once-inferior groups rose to take the reins of power and to rule themselves.

Although these empires easily disintegrated into states, the ethnic mix that commonly populates such structures would not separate as readily. In many cases, the resulting nation-states had to come into being bloodily. The most dramatic of these was the partition of British

---

[*] *First published in OpinionAsia.com on 3 September 2009.*

India into the republics of India and Pakistan in August 1947 which left a million dead and displaced countless millions.

In some colonized areas, the Ideology of Racial Hierarchy was easily abandoned. However, white supremacy clung on, for example in regions like the breakaway Southern Rhodesia (1965-1975). It took its most prominent and disdainful form in South Africa, under the apartheid system that lasted from 1948 to 1993.

In British Malaya, one may say that the separation of Malaysia and Singapore in 1965 was necessitated by ethnic differences, in keeping with post-colonial trends elsewhere.

In order to neutralize ethnic tensions and put them out of play, Singapore took the short cut of strictly classifying ethnic groups so as to guarantee the right for each to learn its mother tongue, and for prevent residential segregation along ethnic lines.

In Malaysia, affirmative action in favour of the majority Malays was implemented in 1970 to correct socio-economic imbalances. However, this initiative has been warped to institutionalize racialist thought over the years, and its time limit discarded. The Ideology of Racial Hierarchy, now backed by religious arguments, thus managed to survive in Malaysia, which thus has the dubious distinction of being perhaps the last bastion of a divisive principle of social organization imported once upon a time into the region by colonial conquerors.

Thus, Malay supremacists can be seen freely expressing their racism in the mainstream press in a way that would lead to immediate and harsh government sanction in most other parts of the world.

Given the historical presentation above, we are hopefully seeing the tail-end of this overextended global phenomenon.

The swiftness with which the discourse of race was thrown into the rubbish heap of history, at least in Europe, was aided by the ideological dynamics of the Cold War that immediately followed the Nazi defeat.

The paradigm of class struggle rapidly and thoroughly came to define international relations for half a century.

With the end of the Cold War in the late 1980s, global capitalism took over as the discursive solvent of ethnic differences, wherewith the absorption of all human economies in the global melting pot is assumed to hold the potential to defuse group tensions.

For now, the main challenge to global economism—aside from its periodic collapses and increasing environmental destruction—seems to be the various forms of religious extremism that have sprung up in recent decades all over the world.

Malaysia's position today in this evolution of political thought is determined by its sad inability to discard past mistakes. Not only did it keep alive the institution of detention without charge or trial used half a century ago against communist insurgents, it has also continued practicing the Ideology of Racial Hierarchy as if it were indigenous to the region.

Mahathir Mohamed once boasted that the West had to learn detention without trial or charge from Malaysia after the 9/11 bombings in New York. Hopefully, the West will not seek to re-import racist discourse from the country as well.

As it is, great interest has been shown by black-majority South Africa in Malaysia's New Economic Policy and its applicability there. Hopefully, the South Africans will be vigilant enough to note the sad tendency that affirmative action that is aimed at benefiting the ethnic majority holds to evolve into counterproductive and archaic racism.

26

No strong MCA without a strong Umno*

UNDOUBTEDLY, the 60-year-old party, just like the United Malays National Organisation (Umno), its senior partner in the ruling Barisan Nasional (BN), has had a long history of conflict. The current split, however, comes when the party is at its weakest; and the BN, the coalition that had always been the vehicle for the MCA's success, is facing the strongest opposition it has ever known, having lost its two-thirds majority for the first time in last year's general election.

One quick look at relevant tables shows that the MCA today has substantial support only in semi-rural and rural states.

Indeed, despite being allocated 40 parliamentary seats by the BN to contest last year, it won only 15. Twelve of these are in Johor, Pahang and Perak.

In clearly urban states like Penang, Selangor and the federal territory of Kuala Lumpur, it was wiped out, with the exception of one seat in Selangor. Urbanity and urban voters are a problem for the MCA, as it is for the BN and Umno.

Given such a thrashing, one would have expected the MCA to suffer an immediate meltdown. That did not happen, partially thanks to its former president Ong Ka Ting retiring and thus taking part of the blame for the defeats.

First published in Singapore's Today and in The Malaysian Insider on 5 September 2009.

However, this paradoxically passed the buck to his successors. With the pyramid of power so much narrower at the top, tolerance for opposition within the party has become a luxury it could not afford.

Mr Chua Soi Lek, the former Health Minister who resigned before the elections in the aftermath of a scandal where he was caught on video with his mistress in a hotel room, received formidable support in the subsequent party election, and emerged as deputy president. He has now been surprisingly sacked by the new president Ong Tee Keat. The old video was re-used to justify Mr Ong's desperate move.

Such a sudden disposal of a popular leader leaves those of Mr Chua's supporters, whose political future depends on their man being ahead, understandably angered. They have vowed to challenge the president's decision. A nasty clash is imminent.

What this reflects is the unease spreading through the party, as it is spreading within Umno as well, that the political future of many who wedded their lives to their party is in jeopardy. The cake has shrunk and its eaters are hungrier.

The MCA's fate and fortune cannot be separated from Umno's. It is, after all, BN that brings power, not each member party by itself.

With the weakening of race-based parties like MCA, Umno and their old ally, the Malaysian Indian Congress, it is tempting to conclude that even if ethnic identity remains strong among Malaysians, the willingness to let personal sentiment decide national politics is not as intuitively given a thing as it used to be.

There are certainly signs suggesting such a development. A row of attempts to rouse racial feelings against the opposition - many done on the front pages of Umno's newspaper, Utusan Malaysia - have had limited success. Even the bizarre use of a cow's head by some Malays demonstrating against the building of a Hindu temple in their neighbourhood failed to anger Indian Malaysians into action.

The inability of BN to regain voter support, as painfully revealed through its loss in all by-elections held on the peninsula since the general election, makes its leadership extremely uncertain about which card it can play.

Should Umno spin itself as protector of Malayness, guardian of punitive Islam or custodian of secular governance?

The danger here is that Umno/BN, left at its wits end, will get ever more desperate. Rumours are rife that Prime Minister Najib Razak is planning the fall of the Pakatan Rakyat government in Selangor.

These are nourished by Mr Najib's expressed wish to bring the state back into the BN fold and his becoming the Umno liaison chief in Selangor. After all, the BN regained Perak state soon after the PM moved in as Umno liaison chief there.

The key question for MCA members to ask today - be they supporters of Mr Ong or Mr Chua - is whether or not the dubious recovery of power by Umno/BN through intrigues will make it impossible for the party to ever regain voter sympathy, and national relevance, no matter who is running the party.

27

BN infighting is just beginning[*]

AFTERSHOCKS of the dismal showing by Malaysia's ruling coalition in last year's general election continue to reverberate through the political landscape. Slowly but steadily, structural reforms are becoming undeniable.

It is now not so much about whether the Barisan Nasional (BN) will reform itself or not, but whether it can stay whole during its painful transformation.

What phoenix – or phoenixes – will rise when the dust settles is the key question? What will never rise again?

The former president of the dominant United Malays National Organisation (Umno), former premier Abdullah Badawi, resigned in March this year; just as Ong Ka Ting, then president of the second most important party, the Malaysian Chinese Organisation (MCA), had done in October last year. This eased internal tensions for a while in those parties.

The presidents of other major BN members, such as Koh Tsu Koon of Parti Gerakan Rakyat and Samy Vellu of Malaysian Indian Congress have chosen to stay put. This has minimized chances for the parties to regain ground support.

The fact that Koh was made senator and then Minister in the Prime Minister's Department by the new Umno president, Premier Najib

---

First published in Singapore's Today and in The Malaysian Insider on 19 September 2009.

Abdul Razak, and not Samy Vellu, has added to the bad blood between the component parties.

Whatever the case though, both Gerakan and MIC have not been able to regain strength from any direction.

The same holds true for the MCA as well.

Recent developments show that its internal struggles are far from over. The fact that neither the MCA nor any of BN's parties on the peninsula has been able to achieve any noteworthy increase in popularity over the last 18 months is putting pressure on both old and new party members alike.

Even where the Have-beens did leave, not enough space has been created for the many up-and-coming hopefuls to unite in optimism. More aspirants to power need to be sacrificed.

And so, each party has its internal problems. However, the BN's big dilemma is much bigger than the sum of the internal struggles of its parts. With all the parties highly unlikely to show success in winning the hearts and minds of young and new voters in time for the next general election, how is the coalition to distribute seats amongst its members to every one's satisfaction?

Indeed, how will smaller parties be able to say "No" when Umno demands a huge increase in seat allocation? And if they say "Yes", will that not make them even more unattractive to voters?

Just as importantly, can BN, whose modus operandi so far had been to absorb parties as these became relevant, give its member parties the sack when these become irrelevant?

With its allies faltering badly, Umno, which, despite serious losses, has the most stable core of supporters within BN, will be burdened further as time drags by. It can carry so many lame ducks only so far. After that, hard decisions will have to be made and the weak and irrelevant will have to go.

The Alliance/BN is the path to power for Umno. It cannot hope to go it alone. At present, the party commands only a third of the seats in parliament. Its reliance on the Sabahans and Sarawakians is therefore crucial, and will continue to grow.

However, a federal government made up mainly of East Malaysians and Umno leaders from the peninsular south is not a stable or viable option.

Umno, or BN, must therefore win back non-Malay votes in West Malaysia if it is to regain any semblance of its former glory. One possible way as far as one can see at the moment – and this is far-fetched already – is for Umno to turn itself effectively into BN, either by absorbing its allies into its organizational body on some way, or by allowing all ethnic groups to join without restrictions.

Through such a move, it would have a chance of regaining the initiative from the oppositional coalition.

Since that is unlikely to happen any time soon, the struggles within BN cannot but drag on for a while, lengthened because they were postponed.

28

Bagan Pinang is Umno's to lose[*]

THE choice of Isa Samad by the United Malays National Organisation to be its candidate for the crucial Bagan Pinang state by-election on 10 October casts serious doubts on the party's insight into the country's new political scene.

Isa's candidature is a slap in the face of Umno veterans such as former premier Mahathir Mohamed and Tengku Razaleigh Hamzah who have been warning the party against reinstating someone who had been suspended by the party for political corruption; and whose suspension was used by the party to trumpet its resolve to check dubious practices.

Before March 8, 2008, such an audacious selection would have passed without much comment. But times have changed, and the Malaysian public is particularly sensitive to arrogant behaviour among its leaders.

Umno would realise this if it were not as self-absorbed as it obviously is at present.

Isa Samad, Mentri Besar of Negeri Sembilan for 22 years prior to 2004, was suspended in June 2005 on seven charges of political corruption. The six-year suspension was later reduced to three after he appealed.

The fact that Umno lost the Permatang Pasir by-election on 25 August after fielding Rohaizat Othman, a lawyer who had been

---

First published in Singapore's Today on 4 October 2009.

disbarred by the Bar Council for misconduct, seems not to have deterred the party from adopting exotic electoral tactics.

Perhaps the significance of that defeat was shielded from Umno by the deliberation that Permatang Pasir was not theirs to win in any case.

Bagan Pinang, on the other hand, is theirs to lose. All the seven by-elections held on the peninsula so far since the general election had involved seats held by opposition parties. This one is the first involving a Barisan Nasional (BN) seat.

There was therefore all the more reason to expect the party to do all it could to avoid shooting itself in the foot once again as it did in August. Now, even if Isa Samad does win, the party will have to pay a long-term price on the national stage.

While Umno may be more able to stand its ground in this case than in earlier by-elections, the constituency's support for the party did fall from a victory margin of 4,411 in 2004 to 2,333 last year.

Should Umno lose in this electoral frontline state where the BN is only four seats away from dropping power, its runs a real risk that PR support will spread further in the peninsula's southern regions.

After all, the parliamentary constituency of Teluk Kemang, within which Bagan Pinang is situated, is held by Kamarul Baharin Abbas of the opposition Parti Keadilan Rakyat. Of the other four state seats within Teluk Kemang, only one – Linggi – is under the BN.

Umno's top leaders are playing a dicey game in placing short-sighted divisional demands before central concerns at this critical time for the coalition.

One misgiving that will linger after the by-election has come and gone, even among Umno supporters, is that this incident illustrates that Prime Minister Najib Abdul Razak lacks control over the party at state and local levels.

This turn of events also shows that other BN members, despite being under as much pressure as Umno is to reposition themselves, are unable to advise their big brother to think beyond narrow party politics.

Whatever the result of the by-election, repercussions within Umno are to be expected. Discontented elements within it are bound to make their objections heard after the battle in Bagan Pinang is over, especially when this year's general assembly, during which serious party reforms are to be announced, is just around the corner.

The party's allies will be watching with bated breath, knowing that their own future depends on Umno's ability to adopt bold and innovative reforms.

29

Imagine no Umno-MCA symbiosis[*]

THE crisis within the Malaysian Chinese Association (MCA) is different from earlier ones because, no matter how it is solved, not having an inspiring message for the young is a greater and more damning one.

This goes for the United Malays National Organisation (Umno) as well.

The fate of the two is inextricably intertwined.

Fifty-seven years ago, the fortunes of Umno and MCA took a quantum leap. In the municipal elections in Kuala Lumpur on Feb 16, 1952, leaders of the two parties at the municipal level decided to cooperate against the Independence of Malaya Party (IMP). In the process, they managed to beat their opponents soundly and the Alliance was born.

Up to that point, these parties - each on its own - did not have the wide appeal nor the internal unity needed for them to claim the right to represent the masses. It was the symbiosis between the two that convinced the British that they now had conservative, anti-communist allies who were sufficiently stable, and to whom they could hand over the lucrative colony of Malaya.

Seen in a longer perspective, what this historical conflation of power did was to lock Malaysian politics into an unbreakable racial

---

* *First published in Singapore's Today and in The Malaysian Insider on 25 October 2009.*

discourse. Though challenged every now and then, this grid has remained in place.

And so, the history of Malaysian politics can be studied through the relative power between the two. Many compromises were made within the context of this relationship.

History of compromises

The MCA under Mr Tan Cheng Lock was from the start more prone to work with Mr Onn Ja'afar's IMP. After the success of the cooperation between the MCA and Umno in the 1952 municipal election, the Alliance could project itself as the effective shortcut to independence. The coalition attracted support, and Mr Onn was deserted by his allies, which up to that point included key leaders of the MCA.

Compromises made between the two parties and the British allowed for sensitive issues such as the status of vernacular languages, the status of Islam, the special position of Malays (which included the unique compromise of defining that community in the Constitution itself), and citizenship rights, to be resolved.

An unsympathetic view of this history of compromises would claim that they failed to satisfy anyone in the longer term. The democratic structure of the Malaysian political system was bound over time to work against the attempt to give concessions made by political parties the status of final solutions.

After a sizeable number of Chinese voters deserted the MCA in the 1969 elections, the Alliance fell apart. The MCA emerged a much weakened partner.

Although it is still generally seen as the second party within the extended coalition, the Barisan Nasional (BN), its status as Umno's peer dissipated properly with MCA president Tan Siew Sin's resignation as Finance Minister in February 1974.

This followed his failure to convince Premier Abdul Razak Hussein to have him succeed Dr Ismail Abdul Rahman, who died on Aug 2, 1973, as Deputy Prime Minister, or as Second Deputy Prime Minister.

The rise of a Malay-centric government, increasingly institutionalised through the New Economic Policy, was too focused a force to be turned.

A new class of Umno leaders with new ideas about the state's role in managing economic development could not be denied.

The BN proved a stable configuration, largely through its ability to centralise power and weaken federalism, especially throughout Dr Mahathir Mohamad's long administration. The MCA's role became less and less prominent, and the dominance of Umno became an accepted fact of Malaysian politics.

With the retirement of Dr Mahathir, and with power at the top being wielded by a less focused personality, the sad state to which the lesser parties of the BN had been reduced became evident. Umno itself had given way to a class of leaders more concerned about their own positions and their own power base than with envisioning good governance for the country.

Denial of the situation continued throughout the Abdullah Badawi period. With no governing party able to project optimism and hope, voters, especially in the northern states, decided to turn their backs on BN in the general election last year.

The situation today is that, aside from an Umno that manages to retain a stable rural base, other BN parties on the peninsula may already have postponed reforms too long.

Whatever parties like Gerakan, the Malaysian Indian Congress or MCA do to reinvent themselves, their chances of attracting members to their diminishing numbers of branches are small indeed.

With the Umno-MCA symbiosis dissipating in light of Umno's hegemony within BN, the closed-door compromises their relationship allowed in the past will be much harder to continue.

30

What Najib seeks is 1BN*

IT MAY be saying too much to claim that Malaysia's major political parties are self-destructing. But they are certainly not in the best of health.

The recently-ended National Delegates Congress of Parti Gerakan Rakyat was a lacklustre show where a well-timed, sassy challenge to resign issued to Gerakan president Koh Tsu Khoon by an Umno backbencher, Mr Mohamad Aziz, had to be brushed aside. The main news from the congress was the proposal - quickly rejected - raised at the Gerakan Youth meeting to discuss the party's withdrawal from the Barisan Nasional coalition.

This came several weeks after Penang Gerakan and Penang Umno agreed to patch up over insults thrown by the latter at Dr Koh, which included the public tearing of his portrait. That burying of the hatchet is not expected to do Gerakan's reputation any good.

Gerakan's problems are a great pity, given how it had started life in 1967 as a strong voice advocating multiracialism, and how it had tried to remain the paradoxical "opposition within the system".

The new discourse in the air is exactly that of multiracialism, and yet Gerakan finds itself on the wrong side of the fence.

Backbencher Mohamad's cheek was also aimed at the embattled president of the Malaysian Chinese Association, Mr Ong Tee Keat, who recently lost a vote of confidence but who has refused to resign.

____

First published in Singapore's Today on 7 November 2009.

The party is now caught up in a leadership crisis that it will not able to resolve for some time yet.

The fourth party in the BN, the Malaysian Indian Congress, is just as badly mired in an inability to renew itself, whether in leadership change or ideological rejuvenation. The appearance of new parties to compete for votes from the Indian community is not helping matters.

This same dilemma is suffered by BN's Big Brother, the United Malays National Organisation (Umno), as well. As Mr Razaleigh Hamzah - nowadays the major internal opposition within that party - has been stating every chance he gets, Umno reforms are not going far enough to remedy the ills it suffers from.

Indeed, the measures that Prime Minister Najib Abdul Razak has been announcing for reforming his administration so far tellingly avoid changing the police, the anti-corruption agency or the judiciary. In fact, he recently extended the employment term of the unpopular Inspector-General of Police, Musa Hassan, by another year. According to analysts, it was disillusionment with these institutions, along with anger over BN arrogance in general, that led voters to move to an unprecedented extent against the coalition.

At the moment, reforming Umno is PM Najib's easiest chore. This was evident at the party's recent general meeting, which was the least rowdy in many years. His hold on the party is undeniably strong at the moment, and delegates seemed to be happily obeying signals from above. So, by most accounts, he has achieved 1Umno.

The concept of 1Malaysia - his vague call for national unity - has been endlessly ridiculed, except in the mainstream media.

With rumours now circulating that general elections will be called much earlier than constitutionally required, Mr Najib's greatest advantage is that two of his three opponents in the Pakatan Rakyat (PR) coalition are showing bad cracks.

Parti Islam SeMalaysia (PAS) remains torn by disagreements about the role of religion in policy making, while Parti Keadilan Rakyat (PKR) is suffering internal dissent in its top ranks. The Democratic Action Party is the only major party without serious internal issues.

The problems PAS and PKR are now facing could have been predicted, and probably were, even by those involved. But should they remain unsolved over the coming six months or so, a snap election would put the PR in a jam.

Recent populist initiatives by Mr Najib, such as declaring Malaysia Day a public holiday, suggests that such a turn of events is not impossible.

The decisive factor in the end may be about which coalition has the least disunited members, BN or PR?

For Mr Najib, keeping his allies outwardly unified is one thing, but convincing voters that governance has improved is something else altogether.

PR's strategy will be to remind voters that not much has changed within BN parties since the last general election, and the reform of key institutions remains a dream.

31

Another index, another drubbing for Malaysia*

THE release of the Corruption Perception Index by Transparency International (TI-CPI) this week was not exactly news that Malaysian Premier Najib Abdul Razak needed.

For seven months in power, he had been fighting fires on many fronts. But the opposition parties are holding up better than expected despite Najib's (mitigated) success in winning back Perak state.

His coalition has not been doing too well at by-elections, and some of his allies are showing signs of disintegration; the economy refuses to impress foreign investors; and most important of all, his efforts at reforms have failed to excite the general population.

His time in power has also been badly coloured by the dubious methods of the Malaysian Anti-Corruption Commission (MACC), and the tragic death of DAP political aide Teoh Beng Hock while being held by the MACC. The commission's tendency to investigate opposition personalities despite the small sums usually involved instead of persons connected to the Barisan Nasional where the sums concerned are astronomical has been glaring.

This, among other things, has greatly affected how the world views Malaysia's standard of governance.

---

* First published in Singapore's Today 21 November 2009.

Where financial corruption is concerned, official foot-dragging around the case of the Port Klang Free Trade Zone - a project where costs had ballooned by six times - has exasperated Malaysians.

What is interesting about the TI-CPI is that it deals with perception. And so, the fact that Malaysia has received its lowest point in 15 years (4.5, down from 5.1 last year) shows us how little impact Mr Najib's efforts have had on public perception of his administration.

This is despite the control the federal government has on the print media, and despite the opposition's inability to present a united front on important issues.

In this year's report, Transparency International states that Malaysia's sharp decline "may be attributed to the perception that there has been little progress combating corruption and a lack of political will to implement effective anti-corruption measures. The MACC appears to focus on "small fish" and opposition politicians".

The country dropped nine positions from 47th to 56th. The fact that TI used as many as nine different surveys to arrive at Malaysia's score makes the result that much more credible, and that much harder for the government to ignore. It was not all that long ago that Malaysia was ranked 33rd. After all, Indonesia, a new democracy, unlike Malaysia, jumped by an impressive 15 spots from 126th last year to 111th this year.

Countries that fell by nine or more positions this time around include Lebanon (which fell 28 spots), Nepal (22), Algeria (19), Mongolia, Bolivia and Ukraine (18), Mexico and El Salvador (17), Paraguay (16), and Senegal, Madagascar and Greece (14). Most of these are countries in political crisis, and fell from low positions to start with.

What is more significant for Malaysia is that when one reads from the top of the chart, the countries that show major falls before Malaysia at 56th spot are only Malta (nine spots) and Austria (seven spots). These three are countries that should be climbing the chart, but are worryingly falling instead. They are not living up to their potential.

This is a strong warning sign for Malaysia, and one that comes despite ample forewarning. Such a deteriorating reputation translates very quickly into a fall in confidence among investors. But perhaps

Malaysia can take heart that for the Asia-Pacific region, it holds 11th spot out of 39th. Or that it ranks third among Asean countries.

Any straw will do when one is drowning.

32

Malaysian Model - What went wrong?*

AFTER the Second World War, former colonies and semi-colonies of respectable size had the choice of either latching on to the global economy and doing the best they can, or attempting to create an alternative world.

For reasons of pride and because of armed struggles against foreign masters, most of them chose the second option in some form. Defensiveness dictated the path nation building was to take.

Nation building for small former colonies and semi-colonies, however, has been a simpler matter. They either grew or they perished. No time for experiments. Economic catching-up was the imperative, and politics had to be geared towards that goal.

It is therefore not strange that in the 1990s, the Asian region was filled with impressive little dragons and newly industrialized countries. They were small, they were light, and they were lucky enough to have avoided holistic political ideology as their nation-building strategy.

All that took a bad beating in the financial crisis of 1997-98. These smaller nations had their figures properly rapped.

What has happened since then is that giants such as China and India finally succeeded in putting aside alternative dreams and have jumped into the global economic fray. For the small countries, therefore, the present crisis has not been as bad as before because the global economy has become effectively multi-polar.

---

* *First published in Singapore's Today on 5 December 2009.*

Now, let's look at Malaysia within this context.

Catching up for the small requires focus. It requires the quick solving of internal conflicts, clear economic thinking, effective use of all available resources, and the manipulation of external sources for one's own interests.

Little Singapore since 1960 provides an easy study of this mindset.

Malaysia had all that as well in the early days. It had a political structure that was strong enough to survive ethnic riots, it had enormous resources, it had strong institutions, it was enviably savvy in dealing with international powers, and it even implemented a radical and innovative economic programme to solve its internal tensions for good.

Today, the economic signs are bad, not to mention the political ones. The big former colonies and semi-colonies have caught up with the small ones, and these small ones all seem to be managing better than Malaysia is doing.

A look at the latest news seven months into the Najib Abdul Razak era gives a depressing picture.

The country is moving in the wrong direction where international indexes on nation building progress are concerned. Falling nine spots in the latest Corruption Perception Index will not help the economy much.

The lack of transparency in the stimulus packages so far has not injected any new confidence into the economy. Along with the endless intrigues to stop the opposition, which have compromised further the already compromised courts, police department, the anti-corruption agency, state assemblies and parliament itself, this has left no one convinced that a serious reform of the system is being attempted.

This was plainly brought home to Malaysians with the recent report that emigration had doubled over the past year. In all periods in human history, people have moved to areas where economic and political conditions are more attractive. In that sense, migration is a good measure of the competitiveness of countries.

The latest news that Malaysian civil servants and students had for years been forced to sit through courses that teach divisive racialism, perhaps explains why migration is increasing.

Politically and economically, the Malaysian model that held some promise in the early years is failing; not because it was wrong to start with, but because the dominant parties have allowed corruption, self-interest, condescension and arrogance to get the better of them.

Malaysia's race-based affirmative action was meant to spur development, not perpetuate racialism.

Indeed, one could say that Malaysia is taking a path that is unique for a small former colony in this part of the world. Unlike big countries like China and India, which once put ideological concerns before economics and which have since then gone the other way; and unlike small countries that has continued putting economic dictates first; Malaysia's latter-day leaders have increasingly allowed racialism and Islamism – and these are effectively ideologies – to be their rhetorical mainstay, whatever the cost to the country's aggregate growth.

The means have become the end. On the bright side, voices calling for reforms – even within the dominant coalition – are continuing. Perhaps there is time yet for Rome's fiddler to stop fiddling and call for the fire brigade.

33

BTN issue is a Pandora's Box[*]

ONE more Pandora's Box was recently opened in Malaysian politics.

The Youth Wing of Parti Keadilan Rakyat (PKR) managed beyond its own expectations to draw public critical attention to the highly dubious nature of courses organised by the Biro Tata Negara (BTN, National Civics Bureau).

Selangor's Pakatan Rakyat government decided to stop civil servants and students who had won grants and scholarships to attend BTN courses where they purportedly endure lectures extolling the inherent superior status of the Malay race and the permanent sojourner status of all other Malaysians. This move was followed by the Penang government, and Kelantan state is considering the same.

The public declaration released a chorus of individual voices regretting their attendance at these courses. Paradoxically, even PKR head Anwar Ibrahim was implicated for participation in them two decades ago. He has somehow managed to fend off criticism about his role.

BTN course had been going on for decades, and although long an open secret, the thrusting into the limelight of this covert method that Umno had been using to propagate its ideology — if one can credit crass racialism with such an epithet — reveals something significant about Malaysian politics.

** First published in Singapore's Today and in The Malaysian Insider on 19 December 2009.*

Can an open secret be suddenly revealed? Obviously; and it is psychologically interesting to note that so many in high places quickly go into denial mode.

This has various reasons.

To start with, there is in Malaysian politics a long tradition for knee-jerk denial by the powers-that-be of anything detrimental to Umno. Here, facts did not really matter. The control that the Centre had over information and public discourse was strong.

A Press that had been obedience for decades is assumed to be unwilling and unable to challenge claims made by top leaders in the ruling coalition, whether baseless or not. A simple disclaimer used to suffice, especially if done by a top Umno leader.

By extension, those who consumed mainstream press information were also assumed to be unwilling and unable to voice disagreement with such claims.

What long-term leaders such as Deputy Premier Tan Sri Muhyiddin Yassin or the head of the BTN, Datuk Ahmad Maslan, do not seem to have grasped is that those days are gone. Finito.

Channels of information in Malaysia are now plentiful, and many of them are not within the control of the government. These have function over the last decade or so in bringing alternative reporting and dissenting views into the open, as is sharply reflected in the celebration of the tenth anniversary of Malaysia's first web newspaper, Malaysiakini.

Malaysia's bloggers, whether serious in their writing or not, have taken politics to a record level, leaving the mainstream media with no alternative but to consider how they are to save their dwindling credibility.

A growing proportion of the politically maturing population no longer relies on the mainstream media for their information. More than that, they are very willing to voice their views.

Apparently, the only people still relying on the mainstream media for information is a select group of Umno and BN leaders.

But what is really interesting is that some top Umno leaders — notably Law Minister Datuk Seri Nazri Aziz and Umno veteran Tengku

Razaleigh Hamzah — who immediately admitted that the BTN courses were archaic and should be closed down or revised thoroughly.

Even Datuk Seri Najib — using his wish to proselytise 1Malaysia — is wishing for the courses to be revised. This signals that more disunity is to be expected within the Cabinet.

Attention is now drawn to the open box. Whatever peripheral reforms Premier Najib and his Cabinet may be able to carry out, however well the national economy may recover, and however badly Pakatan Rakyat fails to put up a united front, the days when racialism was considered acceptable as a pillar for nation building are gone.

As Tricia Yeoh, Research Officer to Selangor Menteri Besar Khalid Ibrahim said in a private interview, "the discourse on BTN being a tool of Barisan propaganda to perpetuate a racist ideology is just beginning; this will bring to light the experiences of thousands of Malaysians who have been through it".

"It is a time of reckoning for Barisan and Umno to determine once and for all what they really believe in and what they actually implement, in spite of all the 1 Malaysia talk."

34

A loosening of commitments[*]

MANY relationships have changed in Malaysia over the last week, and most of them for the worse.

The attacks on churches throughout Malaysia – eight so far and counting – have shocked Malaysia watchers throughout the world as much as it has stunned Malaysians of all races and religions.

What had seemed a problem with largely East Malaysian significance, since most Malay-speaking Christians live in Sabah and Sarawak, became a West Malaysian one when the first church was burned in Kuala Lumpur on 7 January.

Earlier, the Home Affairs Ministry, bowing to perceived pressure from vocal elements within the Muslim community, had signaled through its appeal and its success in getting a stay of execution that it did not accept the decision of the High Court made on 31 December last year that non-Muslims could legally use the term "Allah" as translation for "God" in Malay.

The fact that only one church has been badly gutted while all the rest received only superficial damage holds certain implications. Although it is often wiser to prioritize incompetence before intention as an explanation for irrational acts, one has to account or this seeming failure on the part of the extremists.

A probable conclusion is that these are not hate crimes. It would seem that the perpetrators did not wish to cause bodily harm, and were

---

[*] *First published in Singapore's Today and in The Malaysian Insider on 16 January 2010.*

only following orders or were being paid to throw badly made Molotov cocktails.

What these acts immediately achieve is to change the political scenario quite dramatically. Who will gain politically from it is still an uninvestigated question.

At the time of writing, no one has been arrested. The Home Affairs Minister's publicly declared willingness to use the Internal Security Act over the matter is quite incomprehensible since we are here dealing with acts that are flagrantly criminal for which punishments exist in law. Threatening with the ISA is more an expression of helplessness on the part of an Executive not readily willing to execute the law.

And yet, that is what is needed at this moment – a clear and impartial signal from the establishment that it respects the law and demands the same of all citizens.

The church attacks have definitely damaged the credibility of Najib Abdul Razak's 1Malaysia initiative, now making it practically impossible for the prime minister to have the words needed to convince at least Christians about the inclusiveness of his style of governance.

What may worry him even more, however, is the extent to which the violence and the threat of violence will affect politics in the East Malaysian states of Sabah and Sarawak.

Should his coalition lose control over one of these states, it will in all probability lose federal power.

As it is, with Parti Islam SeMalaysia (PAS) taking a liberal stand on the "Allah" issue, Umno is strangely enough, despite its long-term incumbency, occupying the fringe where inclusive politics are concerned. Silence so far from its coalition allies confirms public suspicion that these no longer have convictions that are not sanctioned by Umno.

Shock over the attacks has also brought many liberal Muslim voices to the fore, and this may yet discourage Malay politicians from keeping the issue alive in hope of political gains. Even the Islamic Society of North America has called for Malaysian Muslims to allow Christians to use the word "Allah".

Where the economy is concerned, the recent events are not welcome news. The latest series of bad press comes at a time when the figures for 2009 report that Malaysia's foreign exchange reserves had fallen by an amazing 25%, with the economy becoming more and more dependent on government stimulus as private investments fall behind public investments.

Most tragic is the relationship between Malaysians and Malaysia. Official figures for 2007 showed that 139,696 Malaysians had moved overseas for various reasons. Data recently released by the Foreign Affairs Ministry recorded 304,358 Malaysians leaving the country between March 2008 and August 2009. Even after allowing for the longer period for the latter figure, the increase in migration is shocking.

By tying language to religion, and thus signaling that the national language of Bahasa Melayu is not totally a neutral medium of communication, Umno has inserted a new and unnecessary wedge into the midst of already badly segregated ethnicities in the country.

In a word, a lot of trust that had taken decades to build up is fast disappearing. With the establishment trapped in divisive discourses despite its own talk of a united Malaysia, more than piecemeal reforms are needed if the country is to reverse its sad fortunes.

35

Middle Malaysia vs One Malaysia[*]

THE to-use-or-not-to-use-Allah controversy and the attacks on places of worship are definitely conjoined events for one special reason - together they show where the government's habit of muffling whatever voices it does not like to hear has led.

It should not really surprise anyone that the increasing restriction on public space through a barrage of laws, warnings, regulations and fatwas has precipitated a conflict that has confused most people.

Should a certain religious word be allowed to be used by a certain group of people in a certain context, given the infinitesimal possibility that members of another clearly defined group of people who would normally not be found in that context, may become confused by that usage to the extent of slipping into a personal crisis of faith?

Try explaining that dilemma to non-Malaysians, in whichever language. It is no wonder that the world press is still trying to get their heads around it, and can't make head or tail of the latest pig-head desecration at two Kuala Lumpur mosques.

Now, whether or not the Catholic Church's monthly publication The Herald is given the final go-ahead by the legal system to use the word "Allah", the government still retains the right to withdraw its publishing licence, which according to the Printing Presses and Publications Act, must be renewed annually anyway.

But events have no doubt overshadowed the court process somewhat.

---

[*] First published in Singapore's Today on 30 December 2010.

The misuse of racial and religious sensitivities as a reason to diminish public space has over time had the cumulative effect of creating frustration; and indeed, the Allah controversy does suggest desperation on the part of someone who feels his or her back is against the wall.

This systemic creeping silencing has been accompanied by a steadily growing gap between Malaysians sorted - or nailed - into different groups whose main means of mutual contact is through controversies.

And so, provocation becomes an effective means of opportunistic politicking.

But still, there are reasons to stay positive. The successive strangling of political discussion has now come to a point where its consequences are overly shocking and are not acceptable to most Malaysians.

At least three occurrences require attention if we are to understand where Malaysia's national discourse is going from here.

Firstly, we see how the Islamist Parti Islam SeMalaysia (PAS), despite claims that its ulama faction had retained power despite the success of its "professional" wing in the 2008 general elections, chose to support the High Court decision to lift the ban on the A-word. This has made it appear a party that is more mature than the ruling United Malays National Organisation (Umno).

The significance of their stand is even greater if one considers how controversies about religion had in the past always managed to excite PAS into acting in a fundamentalist manner. The party seems to be seriously attempting to leave that phase behind.

Just as interesting is the way Umno Youth members have been acting. Actually, they have not been acting, and that is certainly thanks to their leader Khairy Jamaluddin, who has called for calm and who has condemned the attacks on churches. Again, in the old days, members of this Umno wing would have been in the forefront "championing" race, religion and what not.

Thirdly, the concept of "Middle Malaysia" has been injected into the public sphere by Penang's Chief Minister, Mr Lim Guan Eng. He introduced the term at the recent convention of the Democratic Action

Party (DAP), causing eyebrows to be raised in the process, some in thought and some in confusion.

The reason Prime Minister Najib Abdul Razak's "One Malaysia" has been failing as a call to action is that it wishes to embrace all without conjuring the image of a united country. At a time when divisions cut deep in Malaysia, the notion has not been taken seriously.

"Middle Malaysia" has the advantage of being open-ended since its defining embrace extends from the middle outwards and not from the fringes inwards, and can appeal to tentative groups such as "The Middle Class", the Moderates of all colours, the non-extremists, open-minded Malaysians, and even the fence-sitters. Basically, it denotes the country's middle ground.

The DAP's replacement of "Malaysian Malaysia", which is laden with historical baggage, is in many ways a worthy and timely response to its ally, PAS's new liberal stand.

The issue now is, how will the federal government play this new hand?

36

A severe test for Pakatan Rakyat*

IT IS a strange trial taking place in Malaysia at the moment; strange because no matter what the verdict turns out to be, the public perception of what is taking place will remain the same.

Indeed, it is impossible for any observer of Malaysian politics to consider the sodomy charge against former Deputy Prime Minister, and now opposition leader, Anwar Ibrahim, a purely legal matter.

The mere fact that his imprisonment and his removal as a parliamentarian, should he be convicted, will make the opposition Pakatan Rakyat (PR) coalition suffer itsbiggest blow makes it difficult for many to believe that no political agenda is involved.

For one thing, this is the second time that Anwar and his family are being made to suffer the indignity of sexually explicit legal proceedings.

His arrest in 1998 for sodomy and abuse of power led to the formation of the Reformasi Movement that a decade later denied the Barisan Nasional (BN) its traditional two-thirds majority in Parliament.

This time around, there will no doubt be demonstrations should he be jailed but these will hardly be on the same scale as before. This is partly because there was no other way of challenging the Umno-led government back in 1998.

---

* *First published in Singapore's Today and in The Malaysian Insider on 13 February 2010*

After March 8, 2008, the most reliable road to power for the opposition is through the ballot box.

The trial is, therefore, a severe test for the PR.

Mr Nik Nazmi Nik Ahmad, who is a state assemblyman for Seri Setia from Anwar's Parti Keadilan Rakyat, admits that Anwar's leadership is crucial to the opposition coalition.

"We will not allow Anwar to be imprisoned", Mr Nik Nazmi, who was also Anwar's private secretary in 2006-2008, told this writer.

Nevertheless, insider analysts, including the 28-year-old Nik Nazmi, agree that things are essentially different now when compared to 10 years ago, when Anwar was also charged - and sentenced - for sodomy. The conviction was overturned six years later.

Basically, at least four factors are making the difference.

First, a young crop of leaders has come to the fore, consisting of individuals once inspired by the Reformasi and now hardened by frontal battles fought against the BN in recent years.

Many are now entrenched in positions of power. Some are parliamentarians, while others work for the four state governments run by the PR.

Mr Liew Chin Tong, for example, the 32-year-old MP for Bukit Bendera, Penang, and author of the recent book, Speaking for the Reformasi Generation, admits that the results of the general election were possible only because Anwar was there to unite the opposition.

"But post-March 8, cooperation among Pakatan parties occurs at all levels. Anwar's role remains symbolic at the national level, but otherwise, day-to-day relationships cement the coalition in the states that we govern. These ties go a long way. They won't collapse just because Anwar is not there," Mr Liew said.

The second factor - and this may be decisive - is that the shift in the balance of power has made it thinkable to many Malaysians who had feared the uncertainties that must accompany serious change, that the BN can be toppled.

This new mindset is being sustained inexorably by websites and Internet newspapers, which continue to grow in popularity by fuelling the debate that the country's governance must improve if the economy is to grow.

Thirdly, the multi-racial stand that the PR has been taking is being widely acknowledged, especially after Parti Islam SeMalaysia agreed with the High Court decision that non-Muslims could use the word "Allah" outside of missionary contexts.

Lastly, PR's strength comes from BN's weakness; basically the latter's essential inability to project a new image that is not stained by abuse of power, political opportunism, administrative incompetence and racial partisanship.

Ms Tricia Yeoh, research officer to Selangor's Mentri Besar, is certain that the opposition parties will succeed in working together.

"They have been cooperating closely and concretely for two years now, and know that this is actually possible. Sure, without Anwar, the philosophical glue holding them together will not be quite as strong, but the respective PR state governments will continue functioning. The deeper worry for these young people seems to lie, not at the practical level, but at the ideological level," said Ms Yeoh, 30.

Without Anwar, the PR will trudge on because it has to. But it may increasingly be because it is politically expedient to do so, and because power is within reach.

The fear is that the PR's aspirations may soon be overshadowed by the defensive manoeuvres it adopts to neutralise BN attacks.

The PR may begin to lose its ideological impetus. Indeed, that is perhaps what the BN is hoping for.

37

Federalism going down the toilet*

SOMETHING that Malaysians have had to realise in recent months is that political power in the country has over the years become so centralised that local governance is in real danger of disappearing altogether.

Even the collection of solid waste - something one would think is best managed at the local level - is now under the control of the federal government.

Centralism, by its very nature, distances power from the people. In the process, it increasingly brings benefits to those with ties to the central government.

One could in fact argue that the voter revolt against the Barisan Nasional in 2008 was a collective rejection of the ills of political centralism, and that it intuitively sought to force that unhealthy situation to the surface.

That, it has succeeded in doing.

After the egalitarian Malayan Union failed in 1946, federalism emerged as the best structure for accommodating the country's diverse political traditions and socio-economic structures. And so, the Federation of Malaya was born in 1948. This layered configuration of power also made it so easy for the polity to expand into Malaysia in 1963.

** First published in Singapore's Today on 27 February 2010.*

But centralist tendencies had always lurked within this conception. And this tendency took concrete form after May 13, 1969. The New Economic Policy's attempt to balance racialist concerns with economic development was a commendable effort, but one that was bound to fail. It ended up enhancing racial and religious divisions instead.

More than that, it allowed racialism to become the de facto federal ideology. And with that federal government growing more centralist by the year, especially under Dr Mahathir Mohamad, racialism provided the excuse for the country's institutions to discard not only principles of accountability and transparency, but also federalist principles as well.

Racial complicity in the civil service - and in the rest of society - was encouraged. Governance had to suffer in the long run, and notions of justice and the common good were replaced by racialist bullying and political arbitrariness.

The present spate over the right of certain states to 5 per cent of the revenues received from petroleum extracted off their coasts is but one of many symptoms of centralism having overshadowed federalism.

Petronas, the national petroleum company, had been making 5 per cent payments to Terengganu state since 1978, but stopped these abruptly after Parti Islam SeMalaysia (PAS) took over the state in 1999. Payments subsequently made after that state came back to the BN fold in 2004 have been titled "compassionate payments". Sarawak and Sabah are other states with rights to petroleum revenues.

Kelantan, the eternal opposition state, is now demanding their 5 per cent share, interestingly championed by the founder of Petronas, Mr Razaleigh Hamzah, who is also Umno's Member of Parliament for Gua Musang in Kelantan.

The Kelantan prince has lately become the major voice of dissent within the ruling federal coalition.

By pushing this issue, Mr Razaleigh, along with opposition leaders, is doing nothing less than continuing the uncovering of the centralism that has crept so deeply into Malaysian governance since the '70s.

Indeed, it can be argued that the divisions in Malaysia, often seen to be racial or religious in character, is due largely to excessive centralism, and, as in the case of Kelantan, to the unequal distribution of wealth.

Now, when centralism is challenged, signs of the conflict become evident. These range from serious matters such as eager police investigations into every report made against Mr Lim Guan Eng, the Chief Minister of opposition-run Penang state, to more laughable ones such as the case of federal toilets.

Outside a public toilet recently constructed off the main road at Hillside Tanjong Bunga in Penang stands a sign that is as posh as the building it fronts is pretentious.

It says "Projek ini adalah sumbangan kerajaan persekutuan" - This project is funded by the Federal Government.

The fact that a central government that returns about 3 per cent of what it takes out of Penang state should make it a point to politicise the simple matter of a toilet being built for visitors to the hawker centre close by reveals how low the country's nation-building ambitions have sunk.

Judging from the irritation this sign seems to be causing among local residents, how the federal government hopes to win any vote at all from this show of petulance is beyond imagination.

38

Pakatan Rakyat's glass is half full*

THE PAST two years have been a unique time in Malaysian history.

After the three opposition parties decided three weeks after their electoral successes on March 8, 2008 to cement their cooperation by forming the Pakatan Rakyat (PR), expectations ran high that Malaysian governance would now have to improve radically.

With five (now four) northern states under the PR, conditions seemed right for policy competition between two opposing coalitions to commence. This would hopefully reverse the hubris, the arrogance, the corruption and the racialism that decades of Barisan Nasional (BN) rule had fostered.

The wind was in the PR's sails. But it soon became clear that such things were not going to change that easily.

For 13 months, former Premier Abdullah Badawi clung on to power. And despite the fact that opposition leader Anwar Ibrahim's threat to take federal power by Sept 16, 2008, proved empty, the BN showed little ability to turn the tide.

The United Malays National Organisation (Umno) attempted to put a wedge between PR members by holding clandestine talks with certain leaders of the Parti Islam SeMalaysia (PAS), but failed.

Indeed, the improbable PR held its newly-acquired positions because the BN remained confused.

First published in Singapore's Today on 13 March 2010.

Looking back, PR was at its peak after Anwar regained his seat in Parliament at the Permatang Pauh by-election on Aug 26, 2008. However, already looming in the background was the sodomy allegation made two months earlier by a former aide against him.

It was only after then-Deputy Prime Minister Najib Abdul Razak took over the Umno leadership in Perak state last January that the BN regained the initiative, in dramatic though dubious fashion.

Through three defections from Parti Keadilan Rakyat (PKR) and the Democratic Action Party (DAP), it managed to grab power in the state from PR.

As if as an immediate reward for Mr Najib, Umno's Supreme Council quickly cleared the way for him, and forced Mr Abdullah to resign by early last April.

As if they knew that the wind would soon shift against them, PR leaders petitioned the King to stop Mr Najib from being appointed Mr Abdullah's successor. They failed.

The new Premier quickly took some highly-publicised moves to release some Internal Security Act detainees, and carried out some reforms to encourage foreign investors into Malaysia. He also adopted a soft line where inter-ethnic and inter-religious ties were concerned. His slogan of One Malaysia, though roundly ridiculed, won him some points, especially among fence sitters.

His party, however, exhibited hardline traits at the same time. This heightened inter-communal tension, which had been fed by a series of events such as the death of DAP aide Teoh Beng Hock and the continued ban on the use of the word "Allah" by non-Muslims, followed by attacks on churches.

Umno's regaining of the initiative has thus been a mixed affair. It weakened the PR, but at what could be great cost to inter-ethnic peace.

While the three opposition parties, despite their troubles, are still working together, Umno's allies have not developed any strategy to regain lost ground. At the moment, a major crisis consumes the Malaysian Chinese Association. Protracted internal strife has led to new party elections being called for March 30.

Despite BN members suffering electoral defeats because of their excessive diffidence towards Umno, they are as yet unable to formulate a strategy that can reverse their falling fortunes.

Big Brother Umno continues to pull the load, and BN reliance on it grows stronger by the day. This situation may yet be the ruling coalition's Achilles' Heel come next election, especially on the peninsula.

Just in time for the second anniversary of the March 8 success, PKR lost its morally important position as the largest opposition party when three of its MPs defected, and it jettisoned maverick Kulim MP Zulkifli Noordin from its ranks for being more trouble than he was worth.

And Anwar's sodomy case continues to wear him down.

But despite all this, PR's great achievement is that it is still around, and it is still governing four states. The thing that PKR and its allies have going for them is their joint attempt to transcend racialist policy-making. This is what will secure for them a strong and loyal voter base.

Mr Zulkifli's sacking, the delay of which was hurting Anwar's moral leadership, acts as a clear sign that the PKR is prepared to stick to its pluralistic agenda.

To mark the second anniversary of the March 8 "political tsunami", the DAP, PAS and PKR released a report showcasing their performance. Whether this report is accurate or not, the mere fact that they are still working together against headwinds tips the overall judgment in their favour.

The PR's glass is half full, not half empty.

39

How Najib is like Obama[*]

NAJIB Razak became Prime Minister of Malaysia on April 3 last year, only three months after Barack Obama became the most powerful man in the world. While I'll admit that the historical connection drawn here between the two is shallow in many ways, there is some cogency in the parallel.

If nothing else, the two events boded the promise of political change for both countries, and both men took over from leaders who had disappointed the electorate deeply.

While Mr Obama's rise to power embodied the change that was coming to the United States, Mr Najib's taking of office was not due to any promise of reform in Malaysia on his part, but was instead the result of previous Premier Abdullah Badawi's failure to respond to heightened political consciousness among voters.

Mr Najib's is thus basically a conservative regime on the defensive and any reform it implements is not done on grounds of principle. This failure to repackage itself explains the string of strange events taking place in Malaysian politics today.

Instead of acknowledging the public disappointment with Barisan Nasional (BN) governance and addressing its source, his government attacks those seen as having benefited politically from the BN's failings.

** First published in Singapore's Today on 27 March 2010.*

The legal and procedural harassment of top opposition leaders like Lim Guan Eng and Anwar Ibrahim, in particular, misses the point. The people are still disappointed with BN's rule.

Hacking away at the tallest trees in the forest will not make the woods any smaller. This may sound glib but power emanates in the last analysis from society at large; the forest has to be won over and this is something that the federal government has not been able to do in any convincing, systematic way.

BN allies have been astoundingly clueless as to how they are to regain their former status. This comes from decades of diffidence vis-a-vis Big Brother Umno (the United Malays National Organisation), and any initiative the Malaysian Chinese Association, Gerakan or the Malaysian Indian Congress wish to take has to be cleared by a weakened Umno, led by a disoriented Prime Minister.

And without its allies, Umno cannot stay in power, at least not in a functioning democracy. Furthermore, abuse of the law for blatantly political ends will quickly undermine whatever little integrity is still enjoyed by the police, the public prosecutors, the judges or the BN.

In the meantime, Umno under Mr Najib continues to act in desperation. Playing up the "Allah issue" and whipping women for illicit sex have failed to drive a wedge between the Parti Islam SeMalaysia and the Democratic Action Party. The postponement of the reading of the Goods and Services Tax Bill recently is another case in point - any substantive measure Mr Najib wishes to take meets strong resistance from his own power base.

Initiatives against Anwar Ibrahim's Parti Keadilan Rakyat have no doubt reaped some success but resignations from the party by certain MPs have further undermined public trust in the political system and may not have helped BN in any substantive way.

Mr Najib needs a new mandate of his own but does not dare risk an early election. The hidden dangers are too many for him to be confident of victory.

Stepping out of daddy's shadow

This past week, Mr Obama managed to push through Congress a health care Bill that, judging from the ferocity of those opposing it, could shake American society at a very basic level.

In the coming weeks, Mr Najib will also be pushing through a vital piece of reform, the details of which are still unknown. He is to announce something called the New Economy Model (NEM) to replace the heavily-criticised New Economic Policy (NEP) that his father implemented 40 years ago. He is bound to run up against strong resistance, no matter the contents of his initiative.

A clever repackaging of the NEP was once achieved by Dr Mahathir Mohamad in 1991 through his focus on Bangsa Malaysia and Vision 2020. This time around, any replacement of the NEP has to go beyond mere sloganeering - Najib's OneMalaysia has stalled.

Now, when the national coffers are drying up and society's patience is at an end, this new model will have to be a brave and radical one if Malaysia is to have a future worthy of its potential.

40

Muhyiddin mirrors Umno's dilemma[*]

THE shocking and defiant statement made recently by Malaysian Deputy Prime Minister Muhyiddin Yassin that he identified himself more with his race than his nationality reveals the difficulties that the ruling Barisan Nasional (BN) faces.

He was responding to opposition stalwart Lim Kit Siang's challenge to him to state whether he was Malay first or Malaysian first.

First, Mr Muhyiddin was making a public statement with both eyes on his own effective audience, which was not the imaginary Malaysian, but the imaginary Malay. This is clear from his fearful caveat that if he said he was Malaysian first and Malay second, "All the Malays will shun me … and it's not proper". He was hinting that his statement was not an honest one; just a politically expedient one.

Here lies the crux of the matter. Many leaders of the United Malays National Organisation (Umno) have for decades been appealing to their own low opinion of what the Malay ground feels.

This perception is kept alive partly by Umno's need to convince the Malay community that it is basically a helpless lot that needs eternal party protection, and partly by the gap that has opened up between the Umno leadership and the changing Malay community.

The notion that the Malays are in danger of disappearing is the bogeyman that Umno's leadership seems to have trouble discarding. Despite - perhaps because of - the fact that young Malay voters are showing increasing support for opposition Malay-led parties that avoid

* *First published in Singapore's Today on 1 April 2010.*

mention of racial exclusivism, some leaders in Umno are moving to fill the vacuum opening up at the other end.

Ever since Dr Mahathir Mohamad put into words his understanding of the historical, political, social and even genetic weaknesses that faced the Malay community at large in his 1970 book, The Malay Dilemma, and followed throughout his period in power by regular criticism of Malay shortcomings as he saw them, a convention of orientalising "the Malay community" has been sustained as a basic part of Umno rhetoric.

So in that sense, Mr Muhyiddin, having lived his whole life within that tradition, was merely responding as an archaic Umno leader imagines he has to, given the orientalised Malay his party has entertained as its perceived and eternal audience.

The Deputy Prime Minister had understandably also forgotten that Umno controls only a third of the Parliament. It holds power because it has non-Malay allies from the peninsula and northern Borneo. The BN's raison d'etre - often forgotten by its own members - is after all the creation of a Malaysian identity through participation of all races represented through its own members.

That is what Vision 2020 is.

Why the BN suffered bad losses two years ago was of course exactly the growing impunity with which Umno ignored its non-Malay allies and the sentiments of the non-Malay Malaysians.

And the reason why the Malaysian Chinese Association is having such trouble trying to regain relevance is because it had for too long publicly avoided challenging Umno's public show of Malay ethnocentrism.

By stating that he is Malay first, Mr Muhyiddin has basically disqualified himself from the agenda that Prime Minister Najib Abdul Razak has adopted to revive himself, his party and his coalition. This is the notion of 1Malaysia.

His recently-announced aspirations for Malaysia, couched in admirable words in the first part of his New Economic Model (NEM), are aimed exactly away from the conceptual world that his deputy still inhabits.

Indeed, the choice of words was so well done that opposition leader Anwar Ibrahim is accusing Mr Najib of stealing ideas from Pakatan Rakyat. The national discourse is obviously moving away from parochialism and racialism.

In the case of the NEM, all eyes are now on how the Prime Minister intends to translate those beautiful words into effective action that must meet strong resistance within Umno and BN.

If nation building in Malaysia is to succeed, it does not matter where progressive ideas originate from, as long as the goal is to create a harmonious Malaysia that places nationality before race.

I would aim higher. Malaysia can best realise its pluralistic potential if its people can think of themselves, first as sapient humans, then as nationalists, and only after that as narrow parochial beings.

41

Is the Malaysian Chinese Association able to give up race-based politics?*

ALTHOUGH the Malaysian Chinese Association (MCA) now seems to have survived the worst of its latest leadership problems, some serious questions still remain.

Not surprisingly, all of these relate to why there was a leadership problem in the first place.

To start with, we have to ask why a sizeable segment of the Chinese community, which now constitutes no more than an all-time low of 25.3 per cent (2005 figure) of the population, should still think it strategically sound to play race politics.

In the Merdeka elections of 1955, when the Chinese amounted to about half of the population but comprised only 20 per cent of the electorate, the reasons for race-based politics were quite obvious. Getting citizenship rights in the emerging new nation was naturally a major concern for the Chinese.

Initiatives to make Malaysian politics non-racial reached its height in 1965 when the Malaysian Solidarity Convention was formed, led by Singapore's People's Action Party voicing the slogan of "Malaysian Malaysia".

---

* *First published in Singapore's Today on 10 April 2010.*

Soon after Singapore left the federation, two Chinese-based multiracial parties were formed - Parti Gerakan Rakyat and the Democratic Action Party (DAP).

In the May elections of 1969, the MCA lost badly, dropping 14 of the 27 seats it had held. The two new parties came from nowhere to win 20 seats, with the Gerakan taking the state government of Penang as well.

By this time, the Chinese community made up just 34.2 per cent of the national population (based on 1970 figures).

As a result, the MCA's hold on the Finance Ministry was lost forever to its Malay ally, the United Malays National Organisation (Umno).

Under federal pressure, Gerakan under Mr Lim Chong Eu joined the federal coalition to share with the MCA the role of representing Chinese Malaysians at national level.

After 40 years in power in Penang, Gerakan lost power completely in 2008, and was replaced by the DAP.

Malaysian politics may seem extremely chaotic and dynamic, but its major trends tend to creep along more slowly than one would expect.

But this quick look at how the three Chinese-based parties have fared over time raises questions about the present stability of the strange race-based multiracialism exercised for half a century by the Barisan Nasional.

As the Chinese population decreased, the Malays have gained in numerical strength. This alone changes the dynamics of racial politics.

The wealthier, more urbanised, more numerous and more educated Malay population is now much less likely to buy into the idea that they as a group are in danger of disappearing from the Earth, or that their real enemy is the insidiousness of other races. Umno is left fumbling for some new idea with which to exploit Malay fears. But the more racialism it stirs up, the more it weakens its own allies, especially the MCA.

The truth of the matter is - and this is the paradox that has now forced racist elements to organise themselves to the right of Umno - the

BN model cannot survive strong racialism within itself. March 8, 2008, was proof of that.

That is the MCA's dilemma. With the Chinese community diminishing quickly, its pre-Merdeka strategy is outmoded and it loses out to parties whose strategy is not race-based.

What other parties have going for them now is that a similar multiracial strategy is being developed within a more confident Malay community that is finding it increasingly hard to accept racialist opportunism among its old leaders.

As mentioned earlier, trends creep slowly in Malaysia. But be that as it may, the need for a new understanding among the races is being strongly felt.

If the laudable goals of the New Economic Model proclaimed by Prime Minister Najib Abdul Razak signify anything, it is because they express that understanding.

Now, let us see if he has enough political courage and sincerity to see things through.

The writer is a Fellow at the Institute of South-east Asian Studies. His latest book is Pilot Studies for a New Penang (co-edited with Goh Ban Lee).

42

Writing's on the wall in Hulu Selangor*

IT IS by-election time again in Malaysia. This time, the fight is for the federal seat in Hulu Selangor, a constituency that the Parti Keadilan Rakyat (PKR) won by a slight margin two years ago.

Therefore, a similar result for or against the PKR on Sunday will not say very much about sympathy swings.

A big win by one side or the other, on the other hand, will need careful and prolonged study. Undoubtedly, a prominent victory for the Barisan Nasional (BN) will be encouraging for the administration of Prime Minister Najib Razak, whose attempts at projecting itself as a government that will reform the country lack credibility. It will also fill its sails for the next by-election, due to take place in the BN-held constituency of Sibu in Sarawak on May 16.

Similarly, a victory for PKR and Pakatan Rakyat (PR) in Hulu Selangor will encourage it to mobilise its limited resources towards winning in this crucial state.

A PKR win in the Malay-majority constituency of Hulu Selangor will put its candidate, Mr Zaid Ibrahim, the former law minister sacked from the United Malays National Organisation (Umno) 16 months ago, back into Parliament. Once there, he will be able to strengthen his considerable stature within the opposition, perhaps for the eventuality of leading the coalition should opposition leader Anwar Ibrahim be convicted of sodomy and be jailed.

** First published in Singapore's Today on 23 April 2010.*

It will also mean that Mr Zaid's past sins will be politically defused in the public eye. Since campaigning started, revelations had been flooding the media about him having been an imbiber of alcohol and an owner of a race horse, and also for having an appetite for women. He has said that was all in his past.

One heavy blow to Mr Anwar is the defection of Dr Halili Rahmat, a close ally who was the party's division treasurer in Hulu Selangor. Dr Halili ran in this constituency in 1999 but lost.

Apparently, PKR's choice of Mr Zaid was one slight too many for Dr Halili. He left PKR to join Umno right in the middle of campaigning. What worries PKR further is that more defections have been announced, including two from its women's wing in Perak. Four days earlier, its assemblyman for Bakar Arang in Kedah left the party as well, to become an independent.

Compared to PKR, where defections have been taking place briskly, its allies - the Democratic Action Party and Parti Islam SeMalaysia - appear stable and united. It is this strength that the coalition will use to bandage PKR's wounds, and to minimise the damage that character attacks on Mr Zaid may be causing.

This by-election in Selangor, PKR's biggest prize in the general elections, holds great importance for the state's Menteri Besar, Mr Khalid Ibrahim. Mr Khalid is leading the PKR campaign, and while a small loss will not hurt his position, a big win will provide much needed validation for his corporate style of leadership.

The ethnically-mixed voter base also provides PKR with a chance to show that its multiracial agenda holds appeal even in a rural area. A loss would suggest that the coalition has been unable to make inroads into Umno's traditional base.

In many ways then, this by-election is configuring the future of the PKR. The fact that the opposition coalition chose to announce its fourth member - the Sarawak National Party (Snap) - in the middle of the campaigning is aimed at raising the credibility and the sustainability of the PKR and to creep-start the Sibu campaigning.

Experts have ventured that PKR cannot make an impact in Sarawak and Sabah if it did not include local members. This latest development will give Mr Anwar's supporters a big boost.

For BN as much as for PKR, the run-up to the by-election this Sunday has scrawled some writing in indelible ink on the wall. Although Umno did not insist that one of its own should be a candidate, it arm-twisted its ally, the Malaysian Indian Congress, to pick MIC information chief P Kamalanathan instead of party deputy president G Palanivel. This was done despite strong MIC resistance.

Unhappiness in Umno and MIC ranks manifested itself in the form of two independents defying coalition protocol and registering as independent candidates. They were quickly chastised, and sulkily withdrew.

How the altered balance of power within BN is handled in all coming elections will be the biggest juggling act that awaits its members.

43

PKR weakness shown up again[*]

AS THE dust settles over Hulu Selangor, what leaves the opposition and its supporters unsettled despite the victory by the Barisan Nasional (BN) being unimpressively small, is what the whole by-election says about Mr Anwar Ibrahim's Parti Keadilan Rakyat (PKR).

The unashamed "buying" of voter sentiments by the BN through big handouts was to be expected; questionable behaviour on the part of the Election Commission was to be expected; and the inability of the BN to inspire its supporters or voters with ideas and policies was sadly also to be expected.

What was surprising was the character assassination of the PKR candidate, Mr Zaid Ibrahim. For many, that was a sign not only of desperation on BN's side but also of a lack of ideas.

On the Pakatan Rakyat's (PR) side, the ability of the Democratic Action Party (DAP) to mobilise its people in support of its ally and draw support among New Village Chinese away from the still hibernating Malaysian Chinese Association was to be expected, as was the legendary ability of the Parti Islam SeMalaysia (PAS) to execute campaigns was expected.

What was not expected was the hesitant entry of PAS workers into the campaign. Insider accounts do not blame this on the BN offensive against Mr Zaid's drinking or gambling habits, as had been reported by the mass media.

---

[*] *First published in Singapore's Today on 7 May 2010.*

What seemed to have happened instead was that it dawned late on PR allies that Selangor PKR was not able to mount a proper challenge against the determined and well-financed BN machinery.

This determination was seen in Premier Najib Razak's decision to press hands and kiss babies in the last days of the campaign. Such acts are most effective in rural constituencies.

What is now worrying PR supporters is whether PKR can live up to its promise of being the glue that keeps all opposition against BN under one umbrella.

PKR weaknesses have been evident since Perak state was lost to the BN over a year ago.

Before that, Mr Anwar's image was badly hurt when his promise to take power on Sept 16, 2008, was not kept; and the sodomy charge that has been hanging over him for months has definitely distracted him. Internal tension had also been evident.

Defections from the PKR during the Hulu Selangor election period were also timed to cause maximum damage.

The choice of Mr Zaid to run in Hulu Selangor was a surprise sprung not for electoral tactical reasons but as a result of politics external to the constituency.

Outsiders are always at a disadvantage, especially in rural areas. Not only was he alien to voters in Hulu Selangor, he was also not the right person to enthuse PKR people to run and sweat for every extra vote. This explains the lack of enthusiasm during the campaigning.

Mr Nik Nazmi Nik Ahmad, PKR state assemblyman for Seri Setia, and adviser to Selangor's Chief Minister, in an interview with this writer, said: "This is a relatively slight setback and we have a far better base than pre-2008 to launch our comeback. Keadilan's grassroots is, of course, not as organised as PAS, particularly outside the urban areas. Yet, DAP as a party is pretty much close-knit without a big grassroots base as well.

"Keadilan's multiracial, big-tent appeal is still crucial for the success of Pakatan Rakyat. What is crucial is for the party to undertake a comprehensive review of its machinery. That is being done right now."

DAP election strategist Liew Chin Tong, who is MP for Bukit Bendera, Penang, does not, however, think that PKR can consolidate properly unless and until Mr Anwar focuses fully on his party machinery, especially its electoral apparatus.

What was obvious to observers was that it was the women who worked the ground much better than the men could. This had always been true of the United Malays National Organisation (Umno) and perhaps it is time for PKR and its allies to take their women seriously. After all, one of Mr Zaid's best moves in the campaign was to take his wife along.

To be fair, the growth of PKR following the March 8, 2008, general election was unexpected and sudden. It was like a barman filling a mug of beer too enthusiastically. What you get is a lot of froth and very little beer. However, in time, the froth diminishes, either by turning into liquid beer or by being blown or scooped away. What you are left with is the real stuff.

44

Closure to May 13 remains elusive[*]

I FAILED to write an article on May 13 in time this year. The days were flying by and before I knew it, May 13 2010 had come and gone.

However, that has turned out not to be a problem.

I have been encouraged now to go ahead anyway and say something post-dated on the significance of the racial riots, by astounding arguments given by organisers of the May 13 rally in Trengganu for "postponing" the event for a while under pressure from Prime Minister Najib Abdul Razak and other more level-headéd Malay leaders, and even the inspector-general of police.

These did not include former premier Mahathir Mohamed, who shocked his countrymen by agreeing to officiate at this rally. He had already caused much shaking of heads after he launched a right-wing Malay group called Perkasa in 27 March this year. Many, including countless ex-supporters, are wondering if getting a platform – any platform – was now his major concern. This seems unlikely, given how popular his blog site is. But then, no other plausible reason comes to mind.

The provocation would have been dangerously strong, and parties on both sides of the political divide quickly spoke up against it. Asking for Malays to "rise" and to unite was one thing, but doing that on that tragic date could not but be understood as the act of someone boiling for a fight.

First published in OpinionAsia.com on 14 May 2010.

The rally's organisers ventured in defence they postponed the event for a while because the "timing" was wrong. The thought that the timing for an anniversary can actually be wrong is innovative and original; it opens up all sorts of philosophical possibilities.

To Najib's credit, he did manage to stop the rally. It was indeed crucial for his non-Malay allies to show some gumption and push for such a course of action.

Whatever the real situation, the whole episode does tell us that the prime minister is facing strong challenges from his own constituency. Given the new discourse that he is trying to popularise to mark his administration, resistance arising from certain Malay leaders cannot be a surprise to him.

The slogans, concepts and constructs he has thrown into the political equation over the last year include "1 Malaysia, People First, Performance Now", the Government Transformation Program (GTP) based on the monitoring of Key Result Areas (KRAs), and the Economic Transformation Program (ETP) for transforming Malaysia into an advanced country. The last is expressed through the New Economic Model.

What is notable about these initiatives are that the federal government – or at least its consultants – does recognize the areas where reforms are needed. To be sure, the opposition has been harping about them long enough. But at the planning level at least, Najib knows that he has to reverse bad inter-racial ties, bad governance and bad economics.

Whether the establishment is already too deeply stuck in the quicksand of racialism, parochialism, cronyism, corruption and incompetence for the government to do the physically impossible task of pulling itself out by the collar is the question.

In the conceptual world of those who could imagine organising an enormous rally to mark the anniversary of the country's worst ever racial riots, May 13 was not a tragedy but the decisive moment when political power was effectively and violently wrested away from excessively liberal leaders led by the first premier, Tunku Abdul Rahman. In truth, in their minds that date would symbolize victories of all sorts that we need not go into here.

The fact that they wished to call for Malays to "rise" on that day was confounding and was a gauntlet thrown down to challenge Najib's aim of winning back the non-Malay vote and switching the Malaysian economy up a gear.

To the extent Najib fails to convince Umno supporters that his programmes are motivated more by dire economic realities than by narrow ambitions on his part to stay in power, he will have to face increasing resistance from groups who see Malaysian politics as a simple battle between races where one or the other must have the upper hand.

It has been 41 years since May 13 happened. What continues to be worth reiterating year after year is that it was a major tragedy, and Malaysians have to find closure to it by agreeing that it was the abyss from which they quickly backed away...hopefully for good.

45

Pakatan chips away at Barisan wall*

IN ANY ongoing race, the one leading for the moment is always at a psychological disadvantage.

This is most true when he is running as fast as he can, and he has no idea how fast the guy behind him can actually run.

This more or less describes the Barisan Nasional (BN) at the moment, after their surprise loss of the Sibu parliamentary seat in the by-election the Sunday before last to the opposition Pakatan Rakyat.

If anything, Sibu was of much greater strategic importance than was Hulu Selangor, which the BN managed to retain last month. There are several reasons for this.

For one thing, Sibu is a Chinese majority seat that was also a BN stronghold, and a victory there by BN would have gone a long way towards undermining the prevalent belief that the BN has lost the Chinese Malaysian vote for good.

What's more, Sibu is in East Malaysia, which is ungraciously described by BN supporters as a so-called "fixed deposit" region where BN's dominance is vital if it is to stay in power after the next general elections. What has become undeniable now is that fixed deposit accounts have a validity period, after which a new contract is necessary. The BN has forgotten what when that deadline is due; and it may turn out that the principal sum is actually borrowed money deposited on borrowed time.

** First published in OpinionAsia.com 26 May 2010.*

Premier Najib Abdul Razak's appearance in Hulu Selangor certainly won his coalition some support among Felda farmers, but failed in Sibu to take BN over the finishing line. He broke tradition both times by dropping in to lead the campaign in place of Deputy Prime Minister Muhyiddin Yassin. In Hulu Selangor, he managed to steal whatever glory would have gone to the latter for the BN victory. In Sibu, he had to settle for the disgrace.

Thirdly, Sarawak is in transition. Chief Minister Taib Mahmud, who has ruled the state for the last 29 years is 74, and is not expected to run in the next state elections. Not only is his age against him, his reputation is indefensibly bad. And with increasing open debate about the excesses of the old generation of politicians, he seems a burden in any electoral campaign, much the same way that Samy Vellu, the president of the Malaysian Indian Congress was in campaigning for the 2008 general elections. Any sponsorship from him at that time was a kiss of death for any candidate. That was also the case with Koh Tsu Koon, the president of Parti Gerakan Rakyat, another BN member.

If we add to this the troubled past of Chua Soi Lek, the new president of the Malaysian Chinese Association, we see a pattern among BN leaders that is too clear to be ignored or erased from public imagination.

Najib, despite being a political veteran, is not turning out to be much of a campaigner either. His unashamed offerings of taxpayer money at by-elections were disgraceful enough when the BN won in Hulu Selangor. But when such attempts at vote buying fail, as they did in Sibu, he merely appears pathetic.

The speech he gave at flood-prone Rejang Park during the Sibu by-election is fast becoming a classic that will be played alongside other infamous Malaysia Youtube videos such as right-wing Perkasa's founder Ibrahim Ali's stuttering "bulls***" interview replies, Information Minister Rais Yatim's arrogance-oozing insistence that a journalist spoke Malay instead of English, or the judge-fixing "correct, correct, correct" telephone conversation by someone who looked like and sounded like top lawyer V.K. Lingam.

In Rejang Park, Najib, acting in archetypal auctioneer manner, not only insulted inhabitants by suggesting that their crime-infested area was really not suitable for a prime minister to visit, he promised away

$5 million of taxpayer ringgit to buy support with the comic phrase "I help you, you help me"; something which most Malaysians who have ever bribed a traffic policeman would have heard often enough.

Najib's undignified behaviour was all for nothing. This time, he lost despite the vote buying, and had to bear the disgrace of defeat that his deputy would have suffered had he stayed away.

But while BN is now forced to do some post-mortem that goes beyond a mere changing of electoral tactics, the race towards Putrajaya for Pakatan Rakyat is far from over.

46

Najib, the stealth strategist*

Mr NAJIB Abdul Razak could not have expected an easy time after taking over as Malaysia's Prime Minister in April last year. The failure of his predecessor's reform initiatives had allowed the political scenario to change to such an extent that his party and his coalition were now in a defensive mode.

This was clearly seen 10 days ago when his coalition lost the parliamentary seat in Sibu, Sarawak, to the opposition.

However, there had always been space for him in at least two areas to make an impression as national leader and reformist.

The first is in macroeconomics, where the effects of regulatory changes - even if they are radical - do not immediately affect the common man.

Here, he carried out some liberalisation of inherited policies concerning foreign investments soon after taking office. Recent figures showing Malaysia's quarter-to-quarter economic growth of 10.1 per cent, which seems in line with growth levels in countries like China and South Korea, has encouraged his administration further.

The second area is in foreign affairs, where he can be far away from the eyes of the watchful opposition and of worried conservatives in his own camp.

One of the great failures in Malaysia's otherwise proficient handling of international affairs has been its relations with its closest

---

** First published in OpinionAsia.com 26 May 2010.*

neighbour, Singapore. A string of sensitive and stubborn issues are involved, from sovereignty claims over small islands to water supply and the use of air space.

One obstinate problem has been the railway land owned by the Malayan Railway (KTM), which cuts a thin but challenging corridor through the centre of Singapore to terminate in the south at the Tanjong Pagar Railway Station. This complicated matter was close to a solution when the Points of Agreement (POA) was signed on Nov 27, 1990, between then Prime Minister Lee Kuan Yew and then Malaysian Finance Minister Daim Zainuddin.

However, negotiations requested by Malaysia, aimed at including additional parcels of land came to naught after then Malaysian Prime Minister Mahathir Mohamad decided not to use "the package approach" to solve bilateral problems, amidst disagreement over when the agreement would actually come into effect.

International arbitration seemed the only way out, as had been the case when other issues such as conflicting claims to the island of Pedra Branca needed solving.

The KTM land matter seemed deadlocked and shelved for better times to solve. But behind the scene, much negotiation had been taking place - and successfully by all accounts. Better times had come.

To the surprise of the public on both sides of the Causeway, the POA is suddenly valid again. The two sides announced on Monday that there was renewed agreement on those points, basically. This time, it looks like things will be carried through to the end.

The significance of this latest diplomatic achievement between Malaysia and Singapore lies largely in their ability to resolve a bilateral issue without involving a third party.

And since the new solution lays the ground for Singapore's participation in the Iskandar Malaysia project, something that was not yet relevant in the original agreement, the ties that this agreement will foster between the two will be that much more promising.

A rapid transport system will connect Johor Bahru and Singapore, making travel between the two places more painless; and the joint development of eco-tourism and river-cleaning is being planned, as is a "wellness township" expected to be launched within a year.

In truth, this agreement carries great ramifications for the Malaysian economy, especially where Johor's development is concerned. This is also where Mr Najib's United Malays National Organisation (Umno) has its strongest support.

In one fell swoop therefore, Mr Najib has gained ground, not only internationally but also domestically. This is regardless of how negative the reaction expected to come soon from Dr Mahathir turns out to be.

Furthermore, this decision to solve an outstanding national issue in a way that will definitely earn Mr Najib bitter criticism from his former mentor will win him much needed credibility as a reform-minded Prime Minister.

Now that Umno is 64

Najib Abdul Razak had been Malaysia's prime minister for 13 months when his party, the dominant United Malays National Organisation (Umno), celebrated its 64th anniversary. This took place on 12 May; but while he expressed confidence over its future, the fact remains that it – and especially its president – faces a string of overwhelming challenges.

These are daunting not because of any singular policy going wrong, but because the dynamics of the times are working against it and because the long-term negative effects of its extended time in power have caught up with it.

This was marked by the victory of the oppositional Democratic Action Party's slim victory in the by-election held in Sibu, Sarawak on 16 May. Not only did this end the ruling coalition's run of victories in by-elections under Najib as prime minister, the constituency that fell was a stronghold of the Barisan Nasional. The result also gave the DAP its first by-election victory in 13 years. As trends go, Sibu was highly significant.

What the dramatic campaigning in recent by-elections also showed was that the federal government, despite its policy to reform governance, was still making use of promises of money to win decisive votes. Furthermore, Najib himself had been actively campaigning, going against an Umno tradition of leaving such activities to the Deputy Prime Minister. This necessarily fanned speculation that the prime minister felt he needed to be the man in front whenever the BN managed a victory.

This may signify tension between the top two leaders in the country. But equally likely, it shows that how uncertain the balance of power in Malaysian politics has become. A victory in a by-election, any by-election, can potentially turn the tide one way or the other.

Using that rationale, the Sibu victory by the opposition bodes ill for the federal government. Sibu is after all the second largest town in Sarawak. Sarawak, along with Sabah, holds the key to power in coming general elections.

Discursively, opposition parties have the edge, speaking the language of tolerance, pluralism, fairness, openness, renewal, and most important of all, of inclusiveness.

And as Najib himself had been advising his followers, change has to come. The option was whether the BN dictates the direction of change, or it is changed by it.

The party is showing the signs of old age, and Najib, taking the idea from news commentaries, is likening his party to Japan's once-almighty Liberal Democratic Party (LDP), which lost power after ruling for 54 years. That is more or less the length of time Umno has held power.

He seems to be trying very hard to dictate change. The question is, in his mission of bringing change without upsetting his own supporters, will he be thorough enough and brave enough, or will he relax and begin to rely on spin to carry him through, the way his predecessor did.

The challenges facing him, and which will not go away, include the following:

1. An emergent and resilient opposition coalition that is to attract a sizeable portion of the Malay vote. This coalition has a discursive advantage that is most evident in how BN rhetoric fails to leave racial and religious taunts and threats behind;

2. Increased activism among young Malaysians, including increasingly urbanised and educated Malays. This is stimulated by newly discovered avenues for political discussion and debate in the New Media;

3. Bankrupted goodwill from society for the BN government. Abdullah used up all the honeymoon time that Mahathir's retirement provided, which was a lot. Yet, Abdullah went from

a record high in voter support in 2004, to a record low in 2008, and then stayed on to oversee a string of by-election defeats;

4. Worsening inter-ethnic and inter-faith relations, which put great strains on his coalition. These are making it extremely difficult for him to win back a substantial portion of the non-Malay vote. Without that vote, he cannot rest assured that he can remain in power beyond 2012;

5. Falling FDI, which is the factor making reform of the New Economic Policy necessary. Otherwise, he would rather avoid riling the Malay ground;

6. Budgetary deficits that continued under him and reached almost 8% in 2009. Subsidies system has to be reformed, GST is being implemented which together show that the government has an income problem;

7. Strong resistance to change within Umno's heavy structure, which is deeply embedded in Malay social life. This was what most probably caused Abdullah to fall;

8. Challenges from older members of Umno, whose political ambitions are realizable only if Najib should fall. Such a fall might result from his apparent connection to certain scandalous issues that have gained international attention, such as the strange death of a Mongolian translator and conditions surrounding the purchase of submarines carried out while he was defence minister.

9. Challenges from young Umno leaders such as Khairy Jamaluddin, who has been biding his time after his father-in-law was retired, and also Mukhriz Mahathir, who will be trying to draw on capital from his family name and his father's stature and support in order to secure a stronger power base.

10. All his Barisan Nasional allies on the peninsula are unable to close ranks after their bad showing in the March 8, 2008, general elections. Internal fighting, as in the case of the Malaysian Chinese Association, or clueless procrastination on the part of the others, show that they are merely waiting for a strong initiative from Umno. This adds to Najib's burden; and the fact that Umno plays the game of being Big Brother even within the coalition means that it does not encourage initiatives being taken by it smaller brothers.

Over the last year, his slogans and initiatives include "1Malaysia, People First, Performance Now", the Government Transformation Program (GTP) based on the monitoring of Key Result Areas (KRAs), and the Economic Transformation Program (ETP). The last is expressed through the New Economic Model, which is an attempt by Najib to provide space for policies that can bring controlled change to the political economy.

In the end, all the by-elections – and the Sarawak state election due by next year – will merely be a build-up to the final contest, which is Najib's very first general elections. That is the one he has to win, and his chances of remaining in power will depend on how he handles these enormous challenges on the home stretch.